THE SCIENCE OF

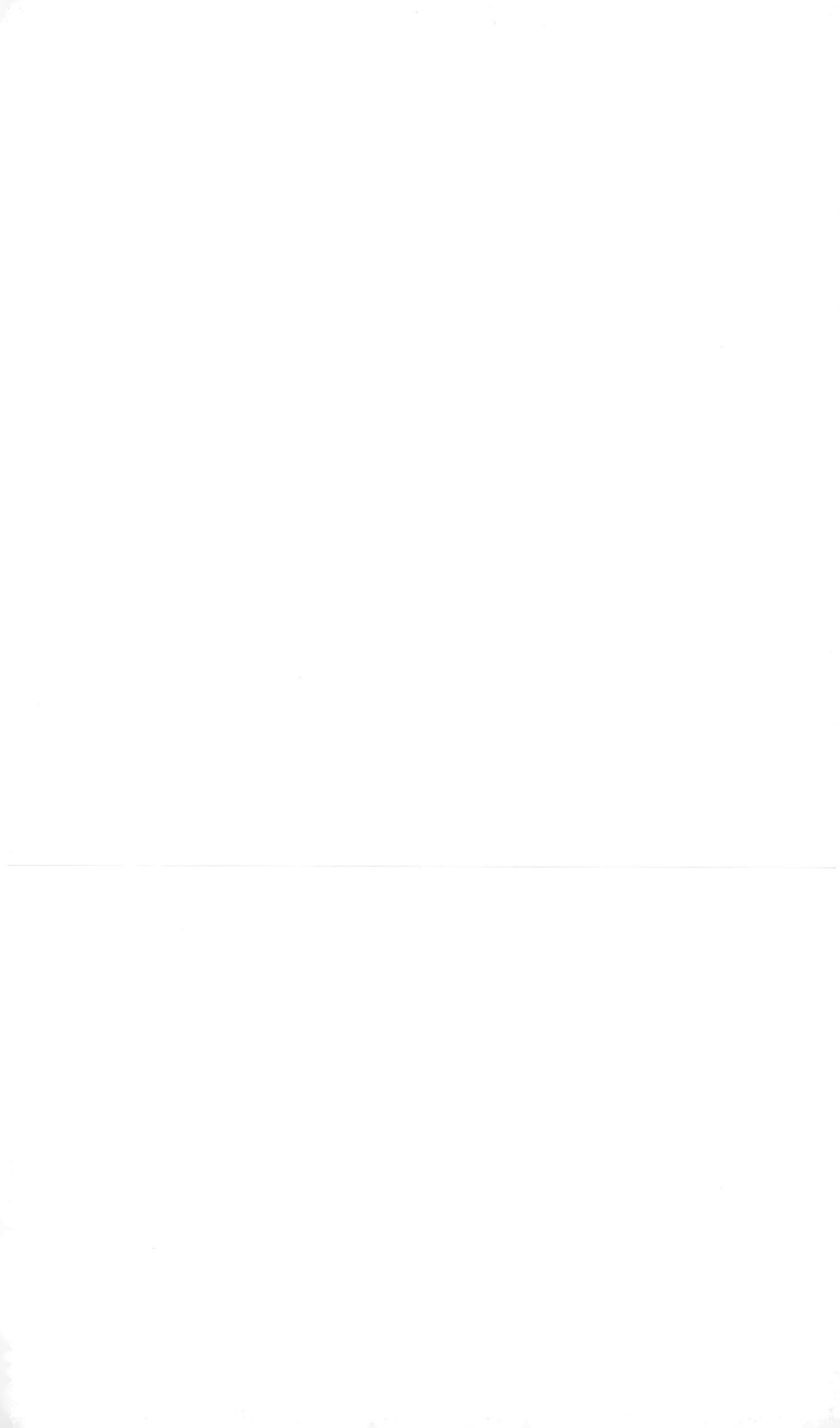

THE SCIENCE OF SCREENWRITING

The Neuroscience Behind Storytelling Strategies

Paul Joseph Gulino and Connie Shears

Bloomsbury Academic
An imprint of Bloomsbury Publishing Inc

B L O O M S B U R Y
NEW YORK • LONDON • OXFORD • NEW DELHI • SYDNEY

Bloomsbury Academic
An imprint of Bloomsbury Publishing Inc

1385 Broadway	50 Bedford Square
New York	London
NY 10018	WC1B 3DP
USA	UK

www.bloomsbury.com

BLOOMSBURY and the Diana logo are trademarks of Bloomsbury Publishing Plc

First published 2018

© Paul Joseph Gulino and Connie Shears, 2018

All rights reserved. No part of this publication may be reproduced or transmitted in any form or by any means, electronic or mechanical, including photocopying, recording, or any information storage or retrieval system, without prior permission in writing from the publishers.

No responsibility for loss caused to any individual or organization acting on or refraining from action as a result of the material in this publication can be accepted by Bloomsbury or the authors.

Library of Congress Cataloging-in-Publication Data
A catalog record for this book is available from the Library of Congress.

ISBN: HB: 978-1-5013-2724-7
PB: 978-1-5013-2725-4
ePDF: 978-1-5013-2722-3
eBook: 978-1-5013-2721-6

Cover design by Daniel Benneworth-Gray
Cover image © Paul Joseph Gulino and artist Kiko Sanchez

Typeset by Newgen KnowledgeWorks Pvt. Ltd., Chennai, India
Printed and bound in the United States of America

To find out more about our authors and books visit www.bloomsbury.com. Here you will find extracts, author interviews, details of forthcoming events and the option to sign up for our newsletters.

*To the storytellers of the future and the beauty
yet to emerge from their imaginations*

CONTENTS

Acknowledgments	ix
INTRODUCTION, OR, SHOULD I SAVE THE CAT AND SEND THE HERO ON HIS JOURNEY?	1
Chapter 1 THE SCIENCE OF INFORMATION FLOW, OR, I SAY SCHEMA, YOU SAY SCHEMATA: TOP-DOWN VERSUS BOTTOM-UP	5
Chapter 2 THE SCIENCE OF CONNECTING TO THE MAIN CHARACTER, OR, WHY DO I WORRY THAT A METH DEALER MIGHT GET CAUGHT?	19
Chapter 3 THE SCIENCE OF CONTRAST, OR, WHY DID THE BIG HUGE SPACESHIP FOLLOW THE LITTLE TINY SPACESHIP IN THE OPENING OF *STAR WARS*?	35
Chapter 4 THE SCIENCE OF EXPOSITION, OR, WHAT'S WRONG WITH AN INFORMATION DUMP?	53
Chapter 5 THE SCIENCE OF CAUSE AND EFFECT, OR, DID THE PACKERS REALLY LOSE BECAUSE I DIDN'T WEAR MY CHEESEHEAD HAT?	65
Chapter 6 THE SCIENCE OF SHARED ATTENTION, OR, IF I WRITE A SCREENPLAY IN WHICH A TREE FALLS IN THE FOREST, AND THE READER FALLS ASLEEP HALFWAY THROUGH, HAVE I WRITTEN A SCREENPLAY?	79

Chapter 7
THE SCIENCE OF CONFLICT, OR, WHAT'S WRONG WITH WATCHING TWO HOURS OF PEOPLE JUST GETTING ALONG AND HELPING EACH OTHER?   93

Chapter 8
THE SCIENCE OF IMAGINATION: TEMPORAL LOBES, HOW TO THINK CREATIVELY, STAGES OF MIND, OR, YOUR DOPE-FUELED IMAGININGS   111

Chapter 9
THE STRUCTURE QUESTION, OR, HOW MANY ACTS DOES IT TAKE TO SELL A SCRIPT?   121

Chapter 10
STAR WARS, OR, HOW GEORGE DID IT   131

Chapter 11
EPILOGUE, OR, GO FORTH AND CREATE   157

References   159
Index   163

ACKNOWLEDGMENTS

Connie Shears extends deep appreciation to Paul for approaching a cognitive psychologist with questions about how the brain processes motion picture information. Quite a journey from our first discussion to this publication! Along the way, thanks to Dr. Daniele Struppa for encouraging the interdisciplinary course we co-taught, *Cinema and the Brain*, winner of a 2011 Co-teaching Award; to Dr. Janeen Hill, for financial and inspirational support from her Dean's Special Budget; and to the many students who enrolled in *Cinema and the Brain* and provided excellent feedback for integrating screenwriting and perceptual processes. Personally, I thank my amazing children—Amber, Sunshine, Jacob, Andrew—for their patience and belief in their mother despite her eccentricities; and to every one of my six inspiring granddaughters for all the distraction, wild fun, and reminders of what really matters in life.

Paul Joseph Gulino extends deep appreciation to Connie for providing the scientific muscle to make this thing work, and I second her thanks to Dr. Struppa and to our students. To this I add thanks to Dean Bob Bassett of the Dodge College of Film and Media Arts for the opportunity to teach at Chapman; to Richard Herman, who shared the vision; to Joyce Bivans, who continues to keep me in the game; and to my amazing daughter Gina who will change the world. And, of course, to little Sasha, who attended many of the classes that provided the basis for this book, despite being just twelve pounds and furry.

INTRODUCTION, OR, SHOULD I SAVE THE CAT AND SEND THE HERO ON HIS JOURNEY?

> Rich and seemingly boundless as the creative arts seem to be, each is filtered through the narrow biological channels of human cognition.[1]
> —Edward O. Wilson

The number of screenwriting books, courses, seminars, presentations, blogs, videos, and Facebook pages seems to be expanding faster than the universe. Advice is everywhere and often contradictory. There are monomyths, heroes' journeys, plot points, seventeen (and also twenty-two) steps, three acts, four acts, seven acts, and no acts.

This book is an attempt to explore the question of whether there is a deeper level of understanding by which one might navigate this avalanche of information—the level of human physiology and psychology. What are the cognitive and perceptual processes going on in the brain of the reader or viewer when reading a script or watching a film? How can a writer/filmmaker exploit knowledge of these brain processes to create more effective, emotionally impactful material? How does a writer or filmmaker know when to follow the "rules" and when to "break" them? And where did those "rules" come from in the first place?

This book will equip the reader with useful knowledge of how the human brain processes visual and auditory information, providing a unique understanding of how movies affect an audience, why successful films tend to follow certain patterns, and what science says about how the audience perceives your screenplay or film. We will proceed by studying commonly held principles: connecting an audience with a main character, exposition, cause and effect, act structure and tension, and conflict—and then delve into the science behind these principles. This is advanced screenwriting based on what science says about

---

1. Edward O. Wilson, *The Social Conquest of Earth* (New York: W. W. Norton, 2012), p. 268.

effective strategies a screenwriter and filmmaker can use, and how to realize them effectively. Understanding the limits of human perception and the unlimited cognitive processes of the audience's brain will help you maximize creative synthesis of these traditional tools.

This is not pre-med. Though neurosurgery is a noble profession, no one need fear becoming one after reading. Our brains, the most complex and mysterious organ of any living organism (yet anyway), all form for one purpose—to sustain life. The era of neuroimaging has made everyone a brain-conscious consumer, if not a neurologist. The intricacies of gyri and sulci—those curious bumps and folds of the cerebral cortex—have been seen in full living color thanks to technologies that now allow studies of fully functioning brains while the brain's owner is still alive and kicking. (Don't get confused by the pictures—a living brain is a dull whitish-gray, no lovely yellows or blues—but just like your screenplay begins with black letters on a white page, neuroimaging pictures are skillfully detailed using various colors to denote structural differences). We have focused on brain functions—not so much on structures. After all, you want to understand how your viewers are going to appreciate your craft, not how the electrons ignite calcium channels in neuronal synapses.

Chapter 1 shows how our brains construct reality not from knowledge of the world but from clues about the world—clues a writer and filmmaker can manipulate to powerful effect. In Chapter 2, we will explore the brain's survival-based preferences that yield emotional connection to characters, explore an evolutionary basis for the notion of character arc and figure out whether a hero belongs in your story or not. Chapter 3 takes a quick journey through your viewer's sensory systems, with attention to how the use of contrast in various forms helps filmmakers and screenwriters avoid the greatest peril they face: putting the audience to sleep. Chapter 4 discusses the uses and abuses of the "information dump," and how you, too, can have fun with exposition. The fundamental wonder of human cognition is presented in Chapter 5, where humans' irresistible drive to understand the world in terms of cause and effect can be exploited to keep the audience following the action. Attention, in Chapter 6, is discussed as a precious commodity that must be managed carefully, and Chapter 7 pays tribute to conflict—why we avoid it in life but can't resist it in movies. In Chapter 8, we shift our attention from the audience's brain to that of the writer and filmmaker: creativity as a life skill that can be practiced. In Chapter 9, we examine a few approaches to screenwriting in light of science, and finally, in Chapter 10, we bring all these various lessons together to see how George Lucas made all that money with *Star Wars*. May the cash be with you, too.

Although this book focuses primarily on the feature film, occasionally we provide examples from episodic streaming or television shows. The perceptual and cognitive processes by which we experience episodic drama are essentially the same as those we employ in experiencing the feature film.

As a bonus, and in the spirit of science, we present, at the end of each chapter, some do-it-yourself perceptual/cognitive experiments.

Ines Adornetti,[2] a philosopher of communication and performing arts, suggests the very development of language in *Homo sapiens* is a result of our need to tell stories (2016). The evolution of our frontal lobes to abnormally huge proportions (relative to the rest of earth's creatures) has been closely linked to our linguistic abilities. Adornetti argues that the need to explain tool use, the temporality of events—before versus after—when some activity must precede in order to change or move to achieve a goal—created a need to verbally explain, to *narrate*. And so from our need to explain, stories emerged, as the distinctly human manner to communicate. We hope this book will itself be a powerful tool for you.

---

2. I. Adornetti, "On the Phylogenesis of Executive Functions and Their Connection with Language Evolution," *Frontiers in Psychology* (2016), doi:10.3389/fpsyg.2016.01426.

Chapter 1

THE SCIENCE OF INFORMATION FLOW, OR, I SAY SCHEMA, YOU SAY SCHEMATA: TOP-DOWN VERSUS BOTTOM-UP

Suppose you are walking along a road and you encounter a large, snarling dog? Your natural reaction might well be to drop your belongings and climb the nearest tree to get out of the dog's reach. Suppose you do so—and shortly afterward, from your perch on the tree, you watch as another person, in response to the same snarling dog, simply claps her hands, *whereupon the dog wags its tail and leaps about playfully*?

You've just experienced the two kinds of cognitive processes that work in the human brain—and which inform many of the chapters in this book. Screenwriters (and filmmakers) who are aware of their audience's propensity to arrive at conclusions based on partial information can exploit it to great effect, especially in manipulating and foiling audience expectation.

Top-Down and Bottom-Up

Perceptual processes—those involving the five senses—rely on external physical stimulation and are termed *bottom-up* processes. The incoming sensory information arrives through your sense organs as raw stimuli—wavelengths of light, shapes, vibrations in the air—and are passed into the neurons of your brain. Stimuli start at the "bottom"—the outside world—and go *up* into your brain.

Gradually our experiences are assembled as memories, with emotions and relationships between various stimuli established in the brain's "experience structures." While there is no single brain location that stores each new experience, there are some key players in structures beneath the cortex—or surface of the brain—subcortical areas with exotic names like thalamus, amygdala, and hippocampi. All that real-world energy becomes patterns of electrical impulses and is eventually organized into concepts and categories. This process occurs

Figure 1.1 Ever encountered one of these? (Art_man/Shutterstock).

throughout our lives, but is especially active in our early years, when the brain is exposed to a virtually constant stream of new information. From repeated experience with real-world stimuli, we begin to know our world, other people, and ourselves. This experience-based processing enables what is called *top-down* information flow and evolves into our own personalized understanding of an object or event. The external world enters our brains through our spectacular sensory systems and is perceived only after our brain compares our stored information with new information flowing in.

Thus our response to the snarling dog was not based solely on the sight of an animal with bared teeth; it was a consequence of previous information stored in the brain's experience structures, information about what snarling dogs look like, cross-referenced with information about what snarling dogs can do to you with their teeth. Our processing starts at the *top*—our brains—and determines our behavior in the world—*down*.

A. J. Cohen, a psychologist from the University of Prince Edward Island in Canada, has depicted the intersection of top-down and bottom-up as forming the *working narrative* in a reader's or a viewer's brain. From the bottom of the model, she presents six sensory sources of incoming, real-world energy, termed *surface information*—this is the snarling dog part of the scenario above. Next, sight and sound—now electrochemical brain activity—begin to connect with our search for meaning. In the model, labeled long-term memory, all our life's experiences, expectations, and understanding feed down, forming a structure to associate what we know with what is incoming: this is where we climb up the tree in our flight from the aforementioned snarling dog. Cohen's CAM-WN illustrates the audience members' brains as they process your movie from bottom-up sights and sounds associating with their top-down expectations, as the cloud in the middle, an evolving comprehension of your story, their working narrative.

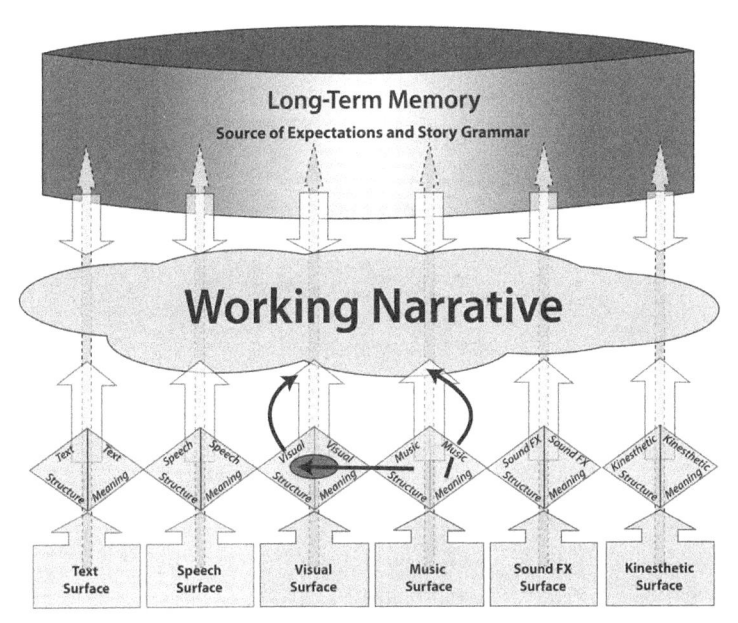

Figure 1.2 Cohen's Congruent Association Model with Working Narrative (CAM-WN).

The woman who appeared after you were in a tree, though, received the same visual information, but responded differently. Why? In this case, her brain contained a piece of information yours lacked—this was *her* dog. She knew from prior experience that her own dog snarled when it wanted to play.

Actually, she was operating under a different *schema* than you.

I Say Schema, You Say Schemata

Although our brains are very complex, they are easily overwhelmed by all the information that comes through our senses. As a consequence, the brain works by way of some significant shortcuts. These shortcuts can be manipulated by skillful storytellers in important ways relating to maintaining audience attention.

One such shortcut is object recognition. For example, the first time you encounter an array of stimuli through your eyes as a pattern of orange and black colors with a distinct shape, these details will be noted and stored in your brain's memory in detail (bottom-up processing). However, once these details are identified as a *butterfly*, subsequent encounters with these stimuli will be instantly recognizable as a

Figure 1.3 If you recognized this object without thinking about it, you can thank your brain's top-down processing. (USDA/ARS).

butterfly (top-down processing) without a detailed analysis. The recognition is virtually instantaneous—a great advantage if your life depends on quickly recognizing a dangerous animal or a possible food source. In addition, your experience encountering a butterfly—warm, sunny day, clouds puffy in blue skies, your caregiver exclaiming "How beautiful! A butterfly!"—shape your object recognition into your attitude and potential behavioral response for the next time you encounter that object. Consider your response if your first encounter with an object is cold, wet, and someone is screeching, "Spider! Squash it!"

So you can see our brain's object recognition is an integral automatic process that intimately combines bottom-up and top-down information flows. In fact, we really don't have any control over our ability to recognize things or people—it just happens.

Another very important cognitive shortcut is called a schema (or schemata—the terms are interchangeable): an organized set of related concepts or objects, usually within a specific *scene*—the word *scene* in this case having a scientific—as opposed to cinematic—meaning (a figure in the context of a background). For example, if you enter a room and encounter a pile of gift-wrapped boxes, ribbons, place settings consisting of paper plates and plastic forks, and a cake with some candles on it, your brain will likely identify the schema *birthday party*.

But our top-down processing has another important aspect beyond the simple recognition of patterns and organized shortcuts: it can affect our behavior. In fact, much of the information we receive through our senses is incomplete or ambiguous, and the brain, as a consequence, is quite creative, actively filling in blanks with assumptions, based on experience (this is known in psychology as the theory of *constructivism*).

The snarling dog you encountered earlier was an object within a scene—strange dog, bared teeth, unattended—and your response was to flee. The woman who played with the dog, though, had a very different response, which informed her behavior: "my dog." Your incomplete information led you to a conclusion that proved to be untrue, because the snarling dog was not dangerous. When new information arises that contradicts a schema, psychologists term this a *violation* of one's schema.

How can the audience's propensity to construct schemas be exploited by filmmakers? Essentially, any time you experience a "surprise twist" in a movie, chances are the filmmaker gave you clues by which you constructed a schema, then violated the schema by introducing information that was withheld from you.

Examples from cinema are innumerable.

Several of the sight gags in the 1984 film *Top Secret* rely on offering the viewer incomplete information, resulting in the construction of top-down connections in the viewers' mind that, with new information, prove to be false (see Figure 1.3).

Figure 1.4 The schema scene here is *office with a phone on the desk in the foreground* (top frame). Soon, though, we get new information: it's a huge phone (bottom frame). The new information is termed by psychologists a *violation* of the schema scene. From *Top Secret* (1984).

Another example of such a top-down construction can be seen in Figure 1.4, from the 1949 film *The Third Man*. The clues suggest menace; the reality proves to be very different.

Frame versus Scene

Schemas, organized sets of knowledge, are set within *frames*—a boundary that allows viewers to see the ominous shadow in Figure 1.4 within the frame of a dark, lonely street. Frames, then, are mental limits, setting expectations based on viewers' experiences (their schemas). When *The Third Man* changes camera perspective revealing the source of the shadow, viewers have had their expectations violated. Such violations of the frame create tension that helps to hold the viewer's attention—which is the primary job of any storyteller.

Of central importance to screenwriters and filmmakers is the second type of knowledge within schemas, known by psychologists, appropriately enough, as a schema *script*—the actions we have come to associate with a particular schema. For example, in our birthday party schema, the frame could be a family home or a gathering at a specific place. The schema script would include actions such as arriving guests, lighting candles, singing Happy Birthday, and opening gifts. However, if after everyone sings Happy Birthday, a gunman pops out of the cake and guns people down, we have a violation of script for our schema: An unexpected action has grabbed our attention (see Figure 1.5).

The opening of *Toy Story* provides a convenient example of a schema script: The clues for the schema *birthday party* lead us to anticipate a series of events to follow: the arrival of guests, the opening of presents, the cake and ice cream. In this case, the events that follow our discovery of the schema align with our expectation; thus, the schema is not violated and there is no "surprise twist."

Another example of a schema script violation can be seen in Figure 1.6, from *Adam's Rib* (1949). At first we recognize the object in Adam's hand as a gun (top image) and the schema script is obvious: he is going to shoot Amanda. Then he violates this schema script action by putting the gun in his mouth (middle image) and a new script emerges: he is going to shoot himself! Finally, he takes a bite out of it (bottom image), violating the schema script yet again. We, the audience,

Figure 1.5 The shadow of a figure on a dark street suggests menace, creating a good deal of consternation for the characters and audience of *The Third Man* (1949). When we get new information that the shadow belongs to one very harmless balloon salesman, the schema frame is violated and we (along with the characters) can safely say "never mind."

Figure 1.6 Spatz Columbo (George Raft) has more than his schema script violated in this scene from *Some Like It Hot* (1959). Note that while the gunman clearly violates the schema script of birthday parties, the audience in this case was tipped off beforehand about the gunman, thus, strictly speaking, its schema script was not violated—only that of the victims.

then learn new information, which the character had all along: the gun is made of licorice.

A screenwriter who knows how to create and manipulate anticipation on the part of the viewer has a tremendous advantage in keeping the viewer's attention—and interest—for the entire screenplay. Likewise, for a filmmaker, who obviously wants to hold the attention of the audience from opening to closing image.

Figure 1.7 The filmmakers here rely on object recognition to terrorize Amanda (Katherine Hepburn) and the audience before revealing carefully withheld information that allows us all to breathe a sigh of relief—and nominate the screenplay for an Academy Award (it didn't win). With Spencer Tracy. *Adam's Rib* (1949).

Your Schema Is Not My Schemata

Because we all have different experiences, our schemas vary as well. The woman in the first example had experiences that included those with her dog; yours did not. Your birthday party schema includes candles and cake; mine includes bubbles and champagne. How can a screenwriter exploit schemas if this is the case? And how can we construct schemas about places we've never been to—outer space, for example, or Middle Earth?

The brain is liberated from exclusive reliance on personal experience by shared knowledge—a commonality of natural laws and shared cultural influences. Most of us have never been in outer space, but we are familiar with people who have been, and when we learn about what they have experienced, their experiences become part of our own, and thus we can draw on *learned information* to construct schemas of places, or experiences we have not been a part of directly.

We have never visited a galaxy far, far away, but the array of stars on a black sky is familiar to us, as are space ships, and even artillery barrages, based on our absorption of the experiences others have shared with us. And while there is no evidence that anyone has ever actually visited Middle Earth, we can construct a reasonable set of expectations about it based on the clues given to us by the likes of J. R. R. Tolkien or director Peter Jackson about a world they invented whole cloth. Remember,

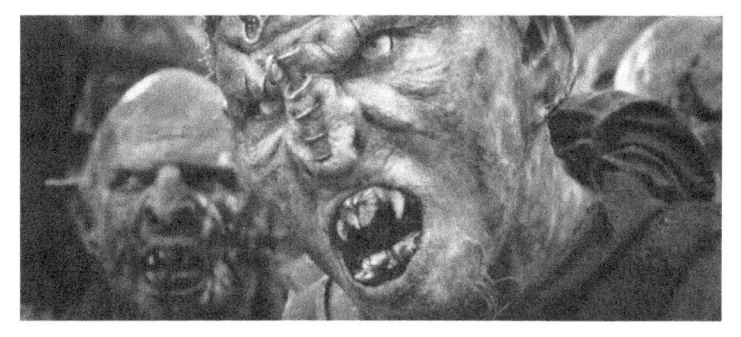

Figure 1.8 Ever encountered one of these? If not, no worries; you can still enjoy *The Fellowship of the Ring* (2001), because the filmmakers provided clues about the fantasy world of Middle Earth that the audience can relate to through both personal experiences (in the case of this orc, perhaps a threatening dog, or maybe an ill-tempered relative) and shared experiences (testimony of others about encountering wild beasts).

your audience is paying to be entertained, engaged in a couple of hours of "this is not real." As experienced movie watchers, we are willing to construct or adapt our expectations of boundaries and actions—frames and scripts of our schemas—even with no direct experience.

The Elusive 100 Percent Foolproof Movie Formula

Because comprehension of a film requires the audience to "bring it"—bring their schemas, created through life experiences, to fill in the gaps—and because each of us has a unique life experience, no two of us will respond to a film in *precisely* the same way. A combat veteran is *not* going to experience *Saving Private Ryan* (1998) in the same way that a nun might.[1] Further, even if a film achieves overwhelming acceptance, the very fact of its existence subtly changes what audiences bring to any subsequent film. Once everyone has seen (or at least heard of) *Avatar* (2009), a movie very similar to *Avatar* will be viewed in relation to *Avatar*—a problem the original obviously did not have.

For these reasons, there can never be a formula for writing screenplays or making films that will work for 100 percent of the people who see them. This is a lucky thing, for if there was such a formula, there would be no need for creativity, originality, or innovation, and the lively cinematic arts would be as dull as formulating aspirin (no offense to any pharmacologists reading this).

The following chapters explore the secrets to predicting a viewer's or reader's response and engagement with your movie or script. Top-down processes are complex and involve many brain areas; but there are some simple general techniques that—consciously or not—successful writers and filmmakers have employed over the years, and theorists have observed.

---

1. This is particularly true of jokes, which are bare-bones stories whose details are likewise filled in by the listener. For this reason, jokes (and comedy generally) are notoriously culture-specific. See discussion in Ted Cohen's *Jokes: Philosophical Thoughts on Joking Matters*, University of Chicago Press, 2008. It's worth noting that the top-rated comedy on IMDB as of publication date—*City Lights* (1931)—is ranked at #34, and thus has *thirty-three* noncomedy films ahead of it. A universally accepted comedy is hard to pull off.

What You Just Learned (or, Our Attempt to Load the Above Information into Your Brain's Experience Structures, a Summary of Sorts)

- Much of the world you perceive is actually "constructed" by your brain. Raw stimuli—light, sound, flavors, and so on—are delivered from your senses to your brain in a stream that can easily overwhelm your brain's ability to understand it all. Your brain thus relies on shortcuts—*object recognition* and *schemas*—to organize and process this incoming information.
- These shortcuts operate by comparing clues from the outside world (bottom-up processing) to concepts and categories stored in the brain from previous encounters with similar stimuli, and making conclusions based on this comparison to what is currently being perceived (top-down processing).
- Schemas—organized sets of knowledge—come with two flavors: *frames* and *scripts*. In the case of a *schema frame*, we see objects arranged a certain way and make conclusions based on the arrangement (e.g., the clues that we recognize as a birthday party). A *schema script* is the sequence of actions or events we anticipate will occur within that schema frame (e.g., guests will arrive soon).
- Because our brains rely on clues—that is, incomplete information—we can be fooled into creating false or flawed schemas, which are then *violated* when more complete information is revealed to us.
- Because screenwriters/filmmakers are in control over which clues are given to the reader/viewer and when critical information is revealed, they can manipulate audience expectations by creating violations. Such violations generate tension in the reader or viewer that keeps them on the edge of their seats rather than dozing or thinking about dessert.

Screenwriting Explorations: Clues and Constructivism at Work

This is a useful exercise in exploiting the audience's propensity to piece together clues to come to an understanding of a situation—and of the writer's power in such a situation.

Write two scenes. In the first scene, a character is doing some activity in one location. While engaging in this activity, he or she sees people going in and out of some other location within sight. This other location might be a building or some other structure of some kind. The character watches these people going in and out, and starts to figure out what they're doing. At last, with some urgency, the character decides to go to this place and investigate. In the second scene, the character goes to the place and discovers what is *really* going on. Can you come up with a twist?

- What visual clues can you give the character, and audience, about what is going on in this other location? Think about props, costumes, behavior.
- What activity can you give the character that expresses who he or she is? This activity may also prevent the character from immediately going in to investigate.

Perceptual Prompts—Perspectives on Where Reality Is

This exercise will demonstrate how our binocular vision (we have two eyes) can move objects in the real world! (Not really, but our brains shift where we see location to adjust for retinal differences.)

Close your right eye. Hold your finger vertically about six inches in front of you so that it partially covers an object in the distance. With only your left eye open, focus directly on the object. Now switch eyes—close the left and open the right, stay focused on the distant object! What happens to the position of your finger? What changes in the distant object? The real world, including your finger, didn't move! But you got a new perspective on available information!

If you repeat this multiple times, studying the details of the object from each individual eye, you get a sense of what your visual system is reconstructing once the transduced light reaches your brain!

Chapter 2

THE SCIENCE OF CONNECTING TO THE MAIN CHARACTER, OR, WHY DO I WORRY THAT A METH DEALER MIGHT GET CAUGHT?

There has been plenty of advice dispensed over the years about creating a good main character for a screenplay. David Howard, in *The Tools of Screenwriting*, says, "A good protagonist arouses a strong emotional response from the audience ... The important thing is that the audience not feel indifferent to the protagonist."[1]

Robert McKee puts the same issue this way: "The audience's emotional involvement is held by the glue of empathy. If the writer fails to fuse a bond between filmgoer and protagonist, we sit outside feeling nothing."[2]

Blake Snyder titled his screenwriting book *Save the Cat!* after a technique used to make the audience like the main character. "I call it the 'Save the Cat' scene ... It's the scene where we meet the hero and the hero *does* something—like saving a cat—that defines who he is and makes us, the audience, like him."[3]

That seems like sound advice, assuming you like cats.

Someone taking Snyder's advice would likely categorically reject the idea of choosing for a main character a guy who decides to murder a man to collect a hundred thousand dollars, or a man who has served time in prison for assault and statutory rape, or a man who starts a business and cheats his close friend out of hundreds of millions of dollars, or who cooks up methamphetamines for sale.

---

1. David Howard, and Edward Mabley, *The Tools of Screenwriting* (New York: St. Martin's Griffin, 1995), p. 44.

2. Robert McKee, *Story: Substance, Structure, Style, and the Principles of Screenwriting* (New York: HarperCollins 1997), p. 141.

3. Blake Snyder, *Save the Cat* (Studio City, CA: Michael Weise Productions 2005), p. xv.

Figure 2.1 Rapist, slacker, violent offender, and beloved main character R. P. McMurphy (Jack Nicholson) in *One Flew Over the Cuckoo's Nest* (1975).

Such a rejection would be most unfortunate, for it would have precluded the creation of, respectively, *Double Indemnity* (1944), *One Flew Over the Cuckoo's Nest* (1975), *The Social Network* (2010), and *Breaking Bad* (2008–2013).

What Life's All About

From a scientific viewpoint, life has one objective: reaching reproductive age and reproducing successfully. For cinema audiences, that means more than that we like to see movies about couples coupling successfully. It means that we are imbued with the capacity to *care* about what is going on in movies.

Many animals have developed socially—into herds, swarms, schools, colonies. The mutual support and mutual defense of such arrangements help creatures reproduce successfully. Human beings evolved as herd animals, too, but our evolution was distinctive because it involved the incredible growth of the frontal cortex of our brains—the seat of advanced, complex reasoning.

Our brain's primitive, subcortical, emotion centers (see Figure 2.3) begin to influence visual and auditory information even before we have actually "seen." Humans have successfully reproduced in large part because these emotion centers intimately interact with our sophisticated reasoning abilities.

The Science of Connecting to the Main Character 21

Figure 2.2 Like humans, buffalo are herd animals. Unlike humans, they didn't develop a large frontal cortex, where the visual stimulus of bloodline relatives was infused with positive endorphins, resulting in close, empathetic relationships with family members. Thus, they really can't be made to care whether Harold Lloyd, or even a fellow buffalo, falls off a clock tower (see Figure 2.5). (USDA/ARS, Keith Weller).

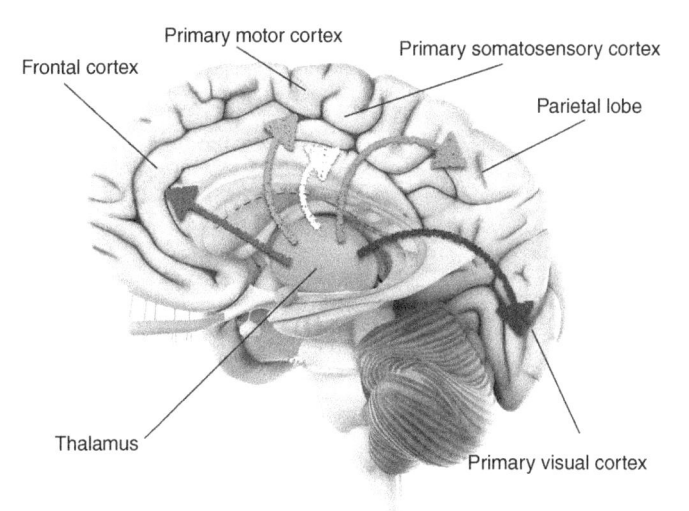

Figure 2.3 The thalamus: Subcortical collection of specialized nuclei that receive incoming sensory information and distribute throughout the brain. The projections from the thalamus pass through language centers before reaching prefrontal cortex; the seat of causal reasoning. (Sebastian Kaulitzki/Shutterstock).

It's an evolutionary advantage for humans to prioritize relationships with bloodline relatives; human babies are essentially born prematurely compared with other mammals—they are completely helpless and dependent on adults for survival. Early on, our emotional centers began to link endorphin release to these close, caring relationships—thus, we *feel good* about family. Almost entirely based on social schemas, our top-down processes will engage in stories that bring relations between characters to center stage.

Extending outward from bloodline relationships, humans developed the capacity to extend emotional connection to others in the support system, paving the way for the capacity to connect emotionally to fictional characters presented in novels, poems, and cinema. In effect, the main character can become a family member, with the same endorphin-infused positive emotional response that a family member generates. Schemas—organized sets of mental representations—that support fast and accurate comprehension (usually) of kinship relations are an excellent tool to captivate our innate preference for successful family relations.

Thus, a story does *not* need to be centered on family—in any typical or blended presentation—but rather like a landscape, a setting against which the narrative finds meaning.[4]

Murray Smith, a film studies professor at the University of Kent, identifies three stages of emotional engagement with characters in a film: *recognition, alignment*, and *allegiance*.[5] Recognition is a bottom-up object or a situation recognized by a viewer—for example, a character chased by enemy agents. Alignment is connecting the new information to the evolving mental representation of the unfolding story—for example, this character captured by enemy agents and threatened with death by spear gun. This is where the audience has existing expectations for main characters, or other characters in the film, and those expectations involve cultural and social schemas. Allegiance is the "survival" basic belief, hope, trust that our heroine will beat the odds against all reason. These three stages map well onto Cohen's CAM-WN model. Look again

---

4. D. Nettle, "What Happens in Hamlet?" In *The Literary Animal: Evolution and the Nature of Narrative*, ed. J. Gottschall, and D. S. Wilson (Northwestern University Press, 2005).

5. Jennie Carlsten, "Black Holes and White Space/45," *Projections* 9, no. 1 (Summer 2015): 43–65. © Berghahn Journals. doi: 10:3167/proj.2015.090104 ISSN 1934–9688 (Print), ISSN 1934–9696 (Online).

at Chapter 1, the working narrative "cloud" is being fed by structure and meaning—recognition, alignment, allegiance—are constructed by your audience, as they search for meaning in your main character's actions or attitudes.

In this view, the audience does not *identify* with the main character, or even empathize. We know that although the characters we see in a film may be in danger or pain, we are not. However, we can fully comprehend what the character is feeling. In this way, our core tie to the character prompts us to "adopt" the hero-he is, effectively, family.

Aristotle and Fear and Pity and Pfaff

Other theories go much farther into the notion that audiences do more than sympathize with a character onscreen; that, instead, we connect on a much more intense level.

In his volume on drama called the *Poetics*, Greek philosopher Aristotle (384-322 BCE) wrote that tragedy inspires the emotions of pity and fear in an audience and, by this means, purges audience members of these emotions.[6] In this sense, the viewer is more than someone emotionally connected to characters on stage or screen; he or she actually *experiences* the emotions of those characters, even though he or she has not personally experienced the actions witnessed. This is actually a step beyond the above-cited advice from screenwriting gurus, McKee advising us to choose a protagonist with whom we can develop the glue of empathy, or Snyder, someone we like. Aristotle is suggesting we actually move beyond empathy and affection into actually, in some powerful way, *becoming* the main character.

Now, Aristotle said a lot of things, including that the planets are alive and move across the sky because of love—an assertion not borne out by modern science. But is there something to this notion of experiencing the very emotions a character onscreen or on stage feels?

In short: *yes.*

Professor Donald W. Pfaff, a neuroscientist at Rockefeller University, has developed a theory in which a human being, in certain circumstances, blurs the distinction between another individual's experiences and his or her own.

---

6. Aristotle, *Poetics*, trans. S. H. Butcher (London: Macmillan, 1902), p. 23.

This springs from the way our brains process the emotion of fear and the sensation of pain. In short, though the emotion of fear is directed by the more primitive brain structure called the amygdala, it receives more refined processing in the prefrontal cortex, where a decision is made to fight or flee: the object or person causing that emotion is only then considered. Meanwhile, the brain structures called the anterior cingulate cortex and the insula are involved in our attention to pain—not only our own, but also the pain of others.[7]

With these facts about fear and pain in mind, Pfaff lays out a thought experiment about how "blurring" might work:

> The theory has four steps ... for example, Ms. Abbott considers knifing Mr. Besser in the stomach. Before the action takes pace it is represented in the prospective actor's brain, as every act must be. This act will have consequences for the other individual that the would-be actor can understand, foresee, and remember. *Second*, Ms. Abbott envisions the target of this action, Mr. Besser. *Third* comes the crucial step: she *blurs* the difference between the other person and herself. Instead of seeing the consequences of her act for Mr. Besser, with gruesome effects to his guts and blood, she loses *the mental and emotional difference* between his blood and guts and her own. The *fourth* step is the decision. Ms. Abbott is now less likely to attack Mr. Besser because she shares his fear (or, more precisely, she shares in the fear he would experience if he knew what she was contemplating).[8]

This thought experiment illustrates not only how one person's experience might merge with another's, but also how human beings tend ceaselessly and unconsciously to be creating narratives—stories—about their own lives, something discussed later in this chapter.

Why would human beings benefit—from the point of view of surviving to reproductive age and successfully reproducing—from this process of *blurring*, or what might be called "empathy on steroids"? The above example was Pfaff's attempt to explain how morality and human ethics might have evolved and may operate. Successful social organization is impossible unless it is governed by behavior that preserves, rather than destroys, other individuals in that society.

---

7. Edward O. Wilson, *The Social Conquest of Earth* (New York: W. W. Norton, 2012), p. 246.

8. Quoted in Wilson, *The Social Conquest of Earth*, 246–7.

Introduction of the Main Character: First Impressions Count

Blake Snyder argued that when we meet the main character, he (or she) should do something admirable so that we like him. At the very least, the introduction of the main character represents a major opportunity for screenwriters and filmmakers generally that ought not to be neglected. Audience understanding of onscreen characters is subject to the *primacy* effect—what they are doing or how they are behaving sets the framework for our basic understanding of the character.

When we first meet R. P. McMurphy in *One Flew Over the Cuckoo's Nest*, he is neither fighting nor engaged in statutory rape; he's dancing and shouting exuberantly after being released from handcuffs. In the course of the film, this exuberant, subversive quality is what predominates in our impression of him. In both *Double Indemnity* and *Breaking Bad*, the main character is neither plotting murder (in the former) nor cooking meth (the latter); both are struggling against physical obstacles in order to make a confession to loved ones, in one case to a close friend, in the other to his family. These more admirable actions are what sustain an emotional connection to these characters when they go about their transgressions during the course of the film and series.

Character introductions (for less controversial characters) that served their stories well are innumerable; a few are worth noting. When we first meet Lars (Ryan Gosling) in *Lars and the Real Girl* (2007), he is on the inside of his dwelling, looking out at the world, but unable to go out and be there himself—initial clues that are consistent with his struggles throughout the story, during which he must free himself from a delusion in order to connect meaningfully with other people. When we first meet Pat (Bradley Cooper) in *Silver Linings Playbook* (2012), he is making a plea to his ex-wife (*in abstentia*) about getting their life back again; he subsequently strives mentally and physically to improve himself. This initial impression is borne out by his actions throughout the film, in which he continues to strive to improve himself to win her back.

None of these characters is doing anything particularly *admirable* during their introductions. However, the choice of moment and behavior the screenwriters/filmmakers make gives us important clues about who these characters are. By discovering very human qualities in these characters, the audience is provided an important link by which it can connect emotionally, quickly.

Introducing Jaak Panksepp

Imagine for a moment a bespectacled gentleman of Estonian descent examining laboratory rats in his capacity as the Baily Endowed Chair of Animal Well-Being Science for the Department of Veterinary and Comparative Anatomy, Pharmacology, and Physiology at Washington State University's College of Veterinary Medicine. That would be Jaak Panksepp (b. 1943), who developed the notion of *seeking* with respect to human response to stimuli. The idea is derived from basic neuroanatomy; that is, our sensory systems all relay in our subcortical emotion centers before arriving to our cortical areas for conscious thought.

Why should that matter to a screenwriter/filmmaker? It's worth understanding that viewers are primed to seek information about characters from a subconscious perspective even before they start to think about your particular story issues. The things we see and hear travel through the emotional centers in the brain, which in turn have been developed through bottom-up information (see Chapter 1) during the course of a viewer's life. When new clues are presented—a man

Figure 2.4 Professor Jaak Panksepp, who pioneered the concept of *seeking* in human perception and cognition. Writers who initially present a character with behavior/activities that express the essence of that character can thereby exploit the human mind's propensity to seek out those clues to create an impression of, and hopefully develop an emotional relationship with, that character. (Andres Tennus).

struggling to make a confession to a loved one—we immediately seek out those clues and put them together into a coherent impression of that person. To the extent that the activity/clues of the character align with behavior we sympathize with—for example, behavior that a bloodline relative might display—we can create a familial bond and thus connect emotionally with that character.

A storyteller doesn't have to present a character saving a cat for us to like him or her, just some activity that we can generally get behind. Although if you're experimenting with rats, having a few cats around might be wise.

Once such an emotional bond is created, the audience is along for the ride, and the *seeking* propensity of the viewer remains in force, engaging the viewer/reader with so-called hook questions: "Is she going to get out of this mess?" "Is he going to get the money?"—questions that arise from your story, but which do not engage an audience unless the audience has bonded emotionally with the character involved. Thus, as long as the audience's propensity for seeking new information is active, they will connect with protagonists' challenges, defeats, and triumphs, because survival is the reward.[9]

This process works even in characters whose predicaments are far removed from our own life experiences. How many people have found themselves bound to a table with a searing hot laser beam moving inexorably toward one's genitalia? Probably not many, but most would likely conclude that the probability of survival (or at least future parenthood) in such a circumstance is very low. However, if we happen to know the person in that predicament—and his name happens to be James Bond—our sense of the likelihood of survival—and the likelihood of some surprise twist that enables his escape—both rise dramatically. In this case, reality-driven audience expectations are dueling with audience knowledge of the protagonist's qualities. This duel, between reality and main character qualities, is a mental state—a duel between bottom-up visual and auditory information and top-down information—*Bond always survives*—which creates the suspense that has led to fifty years of profits from the series (see Figure 2.5).

9. K. L. Badt (2015), "A Dialogue with Neuroscientist Jaak Pankseep on the SEEKING System: Breaking the Divide between Emotion and Cognition in Film Studies," *Projections*, 9 (1): 66–79.

Figure 2.5 If you think he's doomed, you don't know Bond. Connecting to a character unlike any we have experienced in real life can be achieved by reliance on top-down processing. Our knowledge of James Bond's characteristics, and his lifelong pattern of surviving deadly situations, allows us both to connect with Bond emotionally and accept that he's just a bit different from you and me. From *Goldfinger* (1964), featuring Gert Fröbe and Sean Connery.

The Nonhero's Journey

The habit of referring to the main character or protagonist as a *hero*, something made popular by the work of Joseph Campbell and the book *The Hero's Journey* and adapted for the screen by Christopher Vogler in *The Writer's Journey*, can in some ways be a disadvantage for a screenwriter. The problem arises in the impression this word gives a writer, informed, for example, by the first definition listed in Merriam-Webster's dictionary: "a person who is admired for great or brave acts or fine qualities."

For certain kinds of stories, such a main character is appropriate. But for many, it can be an obstacle. As can be seen in the above-cited film examples: neither R. P. McMurphy, the statutory rapist of *One Flew Over the Cuckoo's Nest*, nor Walter White, the meth dealer of *Breaking Bad*, nor Walter Neff, the adulterer and murderer of *Double Indemnity*, fit that definition. For that matter, neither do Lars, the delusional office worker of *Lars and the Real Girl*, nor Pat, the obsessive, bipolar main character of *Silver Linings Playbook*. These people are not heroes in the normal sense, nor do they undertake heroic acts. A writer setting out on writing a screenplay by identifying the "hero" of his or her story is probably not going to come up with anything like the various and very good films inhabited by the likes of Neff or McMurphy, or a series inhabited by someone like White.

Thus, while audiences may respond to stories about admirable people, they are just as likely to be interested in those who commit *transgressions*. Those who make mistakes, get themselves into trouble, do things that normal people don't or wouldn't dream of doing. Doing things that cause them pain. This notion has antecedents in the notion of *hamartia*, sometimes understood as the *tragic flaw* or at least an inner quality that leads a character to undertake an action that leads to tragedy, as derived from Aristotle's *Poetics*.[10]

Thus, it's probably better for a writer to scrap the word "hero" and go with, for example, *protagonist*. (Though, when it comes down to it, if you really want to show off at a party, you might use the term *main character*. The word protagonist, which comes from ancient Greek drama, originally referred to the *actor,* not the role).

Learning from Others: Character Arc

Speaking of ancient Greeks, when Aristotle got around to identifying what it was about drama that appealed to audiences, he decided it was the delight that audiences take in *learning*: "to learn gives the liveliest pleasure … Thus the reason why men enjoy seeing a likeness is, that in contemplating it they find themselves learning or inferring, and saying perhaps, 'Ah, that is he.'"[11]

Meanwhile, many manuals urge screenwriters to obey the dictates of *character arc*, defined, for example, in *Save the Cat!* as "the changes a character experiences as tracked from the beginning, through the middle, and to the end of a screenplay."[12] Sayeth McKee: "The finest writing not only reveals true character, but arcs or changes that inner nature, for better or worse, over the course of the telling."[13] Syd Field identifies "some kind of *change,* or *transformation*" as one of the four essential qualities that seem to go into the making of good characters.[14]

10. Aristotle, *Poetics*, p. 29.
11. Aristotle, *Poetics*, p. 15.
12. Snyder, *Save the Cat*, p. 183.
13. McKee, *Story*, p. 104.
14. Syd Field, *Screenplay: The Foundations of Screenwriting* (New York: Random House 2005), p. 63.

Gulino (2004) has a more elaborate account of the concept, derived from the teachings of Frank Daniel (1926–1996):

> [Character arc] contrasts a character's *want* with his or her *need*, and how the relationship between the two plays out in the course of a story. The paradigm works like this: a character begins the second act with a conscious desire (e.g., [in *Toy Story*] Woody wants to regain his place at the top of the heap) and an unconscious need (e.g., Woody needs to realize that Andy's love cannot be willed; he must accept his place in the hierarchy, wherever it may be). During the course of pursuing his desire, he suffers sufficiently to become conscious of his need and let go of his want.[15]

In Frank Daniel's view, character arc is much more than a simple change in a character as described by Snyder and McKee, but rather a change engendered *in the process of learning*. Daniel also argued that the *theme* of a motion picture is carried by the main character and can be derived from what the character learns.[16] The theme, at least in American movies, tends to be a broad, simple universal truth. In *Toy Story*: one cannot will love. This is not dissimilar from that of *Silver Linings Playbook*, in which Pat learns to let go of his love for Nikki when he realizes he belongs with Tiffany. What he learns might be variously described as "let go of your obsessions" or "live in the truth" or some variation thereon, either one of which is surely sage advice.

In this spirit, a theme can be expressed even when the character fails to learn something and, as a consequence, suffers a tragic fate (mentioned above in the notion *harmatia*). In *Being John Malkovich* (1999), Craig is obsessed with Maxine and demolishes his whole life in pursuit of her. In the end, he fails to get her but never learns to let go of that obsession, winding up in his own version of hell: trapped inside another person's body and unable to look away from the object of his love—even though he will never be able to have her. Craig's tragic flaw could be said to be his inability to let go of his obsession with Maxine; even though he doesn't learn anything, the audience, witnessing his fate, surely does.

The theme of *One Flew Over the Cuckoo's Nest* is more complicated. It is structured as a tragedy (spoiler alert!), but the "tragic flaw" of the

---

15. Paul Gulino, *Screenwriting: The Sequence Approach* (New York: Bloomsbury Publishers 2004), p. 33.

16. Frank Daniel, *Script Analysis* (Los Angeles, CA: University of Southern California School of Cinema-Television, January 12, 1995).

main character is something admirable. He dies because he is unable to give up his humanity: he cannot pass up an opportunity to help someone—in this case, giving Billy Bibbit a chance to lose his virginity. It would be a cruel universal truth indeed to learn if it is to be "Sometimes you have to lose your humanity." The film takes a late turn, though, when the Chief succeeds in escaping and finding his freedom as a consequence of McMurphy's infectious humanity. This turns the theme into something more along the lines of "one's humanity can never really be defeated" or some variation thereon.

The Science of Character Arc

The existence of story itself in human experience is something of a mystery. One thing is true: storytelling exists in all human cultures and there is archeological evidence that it has existed in all human history. Given the precious energy expended in storytelling—for the storyteller and the audience—the question arises—is there some evolutionary advantage conferred on humans by storytelling?

In his book *The Storytelling Animal*, Jonathan Gottschalk lays out the arguments for the evolutionary advantages of storytelling, essentially that stories serve as practice for life. He identifies the "master formula" of stories:

Story = Character + Predicament + Attempted Extrication[17]

This pattern appears not only in stories that humans tell each other, but also in our dreams. In both cases, such stories allow humans to engage in low-risk experiences of life. We are able to learn from the mistakes of others in a more powerful way than by merely being informed: we *experience* being someone else who is making those mistakes. "Just as flight simulators allow pilots to train safely, stories safely train us for the big challenges in the social world ... and like a flight simulator, the main virtue of fiction is that we have a rich experience and don't die at the end."[18]

---

17. Jonathan Gottschall, *The Storytelling Animal* (Boston, MA: Houghton Mifflin Harcourt, 2012).
18. Gottschall, *The Storytelling Animal*, 58, citing Keith Oatley, "The Mind's Flight Simulator," *Psychologist* 21 (2008): 1030–2.

Consider again our feel-good systems, which build positive-feedback pathways in our brains from emotion centers to frontal reasoning areas. These pathways take experience and repetition to establish, but all traverse directly through our language centers. It is no coincidence that from birth, children pursue mastery of their native language every waking moment. Being understood, understanding our providers is the ultimate motivation that makes humans the only animal to use language (at least at the level of symbolic representation). Our survival, our advanced brains, found that communication through language—a shared system of meaning—was the best activator of our feel-good system. Being able to share information moved our successful survival at incredible speeds; and our brains cleverly ensured we would seek to understand by linking endorphin rewards with language comprehension. A good story featuring lifelike dialogue releases an opiate flow that entrenches our positive feedback loops; this, combined with our insatiable search for causal explanations (see Chapter 5) and a main character with whom we connect emotionally, constitutes the screenwriter's golden ticket to audience engagement.

Why the appeal of flawed or transgressive characters discussed above? Obviously, they provide opportunities to show how people who commit social or criminal transgressions face consequences for their actions, and teach the audience *not* to follow their example. And such lessons play a potentially important role in teaching moral behavior, the glue that binds societies together so they can function successfully. "Story—sacred and profane—is perhaps *the* main cohering force in human life," says Gottschall. "Story is the counterforce to social disorder, the tendency of things to fall apart."[19]

What You Just Learned (or, Our Attempt to Load the Above Information into Your Brain's Experience Structures, a Summary of Sorts)

- The science of connecting to main characters has presented some cool and clever screenwriting tools. Good guys can be bad, as long as they are family—a direct result of how *our brains' entire functional purpose is to survive*. Our brains route the new information we are learning about R. P. McMurphy through our *emotion centers*. This evolutionary arrangement in human brains

---

19. Gottschall, *The Storytelling Animal*, p. 138.

Figure 2.6 Harold Lloyd teaches the receptive viewer that it's not good to hang from clock towers (*Safety Last*, 1923). The theory of "blurring" suggests that a neurological process allows humans to experience the fear that this character is experiencing—without us having to be in actual danger (spoiler alert: he actually wasn't in any danger, since there was a mattress on a roof just a few feet below him).

- means a bad good guy—presented engagingly—will be "adopted" as "family" and readers or viewers will connect via survival instincts.
- Aristotle's idea that we have our emotions purged by witnessing those emotions in characters finds basis in neuroscience expressed in the "thought experiment" that *blurs emotions* between an individual and another, by which we can experience in our imagination what another person is experiencing. Which is a lot more comfortable than physical co-embodiment.
- We've reminded you of the *first impression importance* for your protagonist, which does not necessarily mean acts of heroism— although cat saving has its place. *Seeking*—the insistence of the human brain to connect new information with something we already know—raises those *hook questions* in readers or viewers "will she live?" "Who's going to win?" These involuntary brain responses to connect, to seek, keep your audience attending and

emotionally engaged as your main man (or woman) faces the challenges of your story.

- *Character Arc*—what your character learns in the course of a story—has a basis in evolutionary theory—that we can learn life's lessons by experiencing the lives of others in story—without having to go through potentially dangerous experiences ourselves.

Screenwriting Explorations: Empathy

Do a one-page word sketch of the most detestable person you know; someone you dislike tremendously. Provide specific examples of the behavior you find detestable. In the sketch, speculate as to why this person is this way. Now write a monologue, from that person's point of view, describing one of the incidents you described as detestable. Can you begin to empathize? See it from that person's point of view? Such a character can be useful both as a potential protagonist and as a very compelling antagonist.

Perceptual Prompts—Who Is the Bad Guy?

The modularity of our senses (Fodor in Chapter 7) means that somewhere in our brains seeing and hearing combine into what feels like a singular experience.

But seeing is not hearing nor vice versa—try this:
Watch the scariest scenes from *Psycho* with the audio off. Not so scary, huh? Or try listening to a love scene—no pictures—are you as involved with the characters?
Discrepancies in visual versus auditory information (such as the Count Basie Band actually being in the scene in *Blazing Saddles*) can confuse emotional attachment in viewers—sometimes intriguing, sometimes disengaging.

Chapter 3

THE SCIENCE OF CONTRAST, OR, WHY DID THE BIG HUGE SPACESHIP FOLLOW THE LITTLE TINY SPACESHIP IN THE OPENING OF *STAR WARS*?

Way back in the 1860s, German playwright and theorist Gustav Freytag (1816–1895) told aspiring playwrights that a "variation in mood and modest contrasts in color are as necessary to the drama as it is that in a painting."[1] A century later, screenwriting theorist Frank Daniel extolled the virtues of contrast in "sound, color, light, pace."[2]

Naturally, a screenwriter can only, in the strictest sense, use contrast in one way: the black type and the white background of his or her screenplay. Still, through the use of words, the screenwriter evokes the mental images that allow the reader to experience the film in his or her mind. The screenwriter creates the film first, on paper, and in the mind of the reader.

Thus, screenwriter George Lucas rendered the moment in Figure 3.1 as: "A tiny silver spacecraft, a Rebel Blockade Runner firing lasers from the back of the ship, races through space. It is pursed by a giant Imperial Stardestroyer." The writer writes, and the imagination of the reader takes over.

What is the effect of the contrast in the size of the space ships? On a most basic level, we sit up and take notice. We are also brought into awareness of important narrative elements: the power imbalance between the pursuer and the pursued, whose acquaintance we will make shortly.

Use of visual contrast in cinema manifests itself in two ways: within the frame itself, very commonly with what is called low-key lighting

---

1. Gustav Freytag, *The Technique of the Drama: An Exposition of Dramatic Composition and Art*, trans. E. J. MacEwan (Chicago, IL: Scott, Foresman, 1900), p. 44.

2. Frank Daniel, *Workshop Lecture* (New York: Columbia University, October 7, 1980).

Figure 3.1 A contrast both in size and in sequence. *Star Wars* (1977).

Figure 3.2 Low-key, high-contrast lighting in *Fellowship of the Ring* (2001).

(see Figure 3.2) but, more importantly for the purposes of a screenwriter, in a sequence of shots (see Figures 3.3, 3.4, and 3.5). Of course, in Figure 3.1, contrast occurs both in the frame and in the sequence.

Further, beyond the use of contrast in a strictly visual sense, screenwriters employ contrast with respect to creating and releasing *tension*

Figure 3.3 Contrasting sequence of shots: Close-up and long shot (in case you can't tell, the lower frame is a desert landscape). *Lawrence of Arabia* (1962).

throughout a screenplay (and movie). These rhythms of alternating stimulus are essential for two reasons: keeping the audience focused on the film and keeping your audience's brain from being fatigued or, worse, falling asleep.

A Little Science

Nothing is more important than vision when it comes to screenwriting—the eyes are the projectors of the visual world onto the screens of our retinas.[3] The retina, a nutrient-rich membrane lining the inside back walls of our eyes, houses millions of photoreceptors, which, like all neurons, receive information, add specific *neurotransmitters* (a chemical

---

3. R. L. Gregory, *Eye and Brain: The Psychology of Seeing*. 5th ed. (Oxford: Oxford University Press, 1997).

Figure 3.4 Contrasting sequence of shots: Light and dark. *Breaking Bad* (2008).

substance that causes the transfer of the impulse to another nerve fiber), and pass the message along. These receptors actually take in photons—particles of light—and chemically change the energy into neural impulses so the brain can make sense of them.

The photoreceptors are of two types: *rods* are designed to detect low levels of light, so they are particularly responsive to shadows and edges, especially if these shadows or edges are moving, and *cones,* which detect detail and color in adequate light (see Figure 3.5). We have nearly three times the number of rods to cones, which means a majority of our sight is devoted to the darker, less detailed information in our world.

If the audience is watching your movie in the typical hushed, dark theater, you can maximize their visual attention by skilled use of low light, movement, and contrasting orientations.

STRUCTURE OF THE RETINA

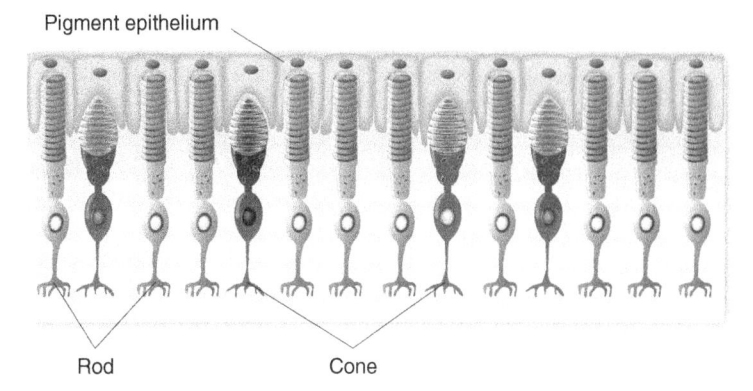

Pigment epithelium

Rod Cone

Figure 3.5 With three times as many rods as cones, your vision is more attuned to detecting edges of objects and movement than color. (Designua/Shutterstock).

Directing Attention

Our eyes move in all directions of course; however, when we hold our eyes still to bring something into sharpest focus, we are directing the center of our retina, where the majority of our cones are located, to maximize the available light in order to increase clarity of detail. This movement is described as a *fixation*, and the duration and location of fixations can be measured. When we then move our eyes to another location (or, in scientific terms, when we *saccade)*, this complimentary time and location are also measurable through devices known as *eye trackers*.

Eye-tracking research has been extensively employed by marketing and advertisement interests to assess success of consumer interest. Recently, this methodology has been utilized to study audience attention and comprehension of dynamic video stimuli.[4] When audience eye gaze was measured, both within and across a screen, it was confirmed that attention (duration and location of fixations) *was allocated by narrative storyline.*

4. C. Christoforou, S. Christou-Champi, F. Constantinidou, and M. Theodorou, "From the Eyes and the Heart: A Novel Eye-Gaze Metric that Predicts Video Preferences of a Large Audience." *Frontiers in Psychology*, 6 (579): 1–11. http://journal.frontiersin.org/article/10.3389/fpsyg.2015.00579. doi: 10.3889/fpsyg.2015.00579.http://dx.doi.org/10.3389/fpsyg.2015.00579.

In movies, it is the narrative that carries viewer's attention, so eye gaze—fixations and saccades—are closely tied to the viewer's top-down comprehension of the storyline. On the CAM-WN model (Chapter 1), this is the layer of diamonds that applies structure and meaning as the top-down experience is consulted. Contrast in light, whether intensity or amount, creates opportunity to direct attention to the integral message of the story. Our visual receptors respond to changes in light, as the rods fire best in low light and the cones require more light to detect detail and color. When a filmmaker understands that as the eyes move to adjust our vision to the light available under varying conditions, the filmmaker also knows that a viewer's attention is also being directed, and when these changes to create contrast in lighting are integrated with specific storyline moments, viewers are attending to those implied or implicit narrative cues.

The bottom line: the use of contrast you see in successful films is nothing more than the manipulation of our perceptual system to direct us to the story elements that matter, in order to help us understand the story—and keep us watching.

Rods and cones are receptor neurons—they receive light and change it into electrochemical impulses—and receptor neurons are demanding, greedy consumers of real-world energy. Rods and cones insist on constant change or they simply get bored and cease firing. This phenomenon, referred to as *neuronal fatigue*, is overcome in general because our eyes constantly move. We are seldom conscious of every saccade or scan, but our eyes dart about the visual scene anyway. Each move alters the light entering our eyes, and falls just slightly differently on rods or cones, thus keeping the receptor cells busy transducing new and changing information.

Another contrast our eyes create is borders and edges, where none exist. Try the do-it-yourself Perceptual Prompt and imagine how creative this can be to the screenwriter whose goal is to puzzle, tease, and keep an audience glued to the screen for an answer.

Neuronal fatigue can be self-induced by starring at a waterfall for a few minutes, then gaze at the ground or still cliff beside it—the ground will appear to drift upward! This well-known "waterfall effect" has been a favorite illusion since the nineteenth century when German psychologist Sigmund Exner suggested that neurons tuned to detect downward motion are fatigued after seconds of nonchanging stimuli and when you move your eyes to something stationary—*voila!* the upward-detecting neurons jump at the chance to fire. More recently, neuroimaging studies have confirmed neuronal fatigue results in visual cortex overactive opposite responses.

Contrast created by breaks in continuous motion also allows our brains to "reset" as it were. Tognoli and Kelso (2014) explain that patterns of neuronal activity are dynamic in viewers while movie watching. These patterns achieve a synchronicity when narratives, characters, and current scene events are all consistent with viewers' comprehension of the story. Transient patterns, shifts in which neurons are actively firing, indicate the viewer has experienced a change in one of these information sources; a lighting change has moved attention, a character action has been in an unexpected direction, or a major premise of the narrative has been violated. Contemporary neuroscience combines nicely with film theorists Bordwell and Thompson (2006) who emphasize the importance of patterns in narrative storytelling in assisting audience comprehension. The patterns of our neurons when we "get" the story are synchronized—when we are thrown a curve, new neurons have to get active in order to update our mental representation of events—this prevents neuronal fatigue and, even better, pulls your audience back into awake, aware, alert engagement in your screenplay.

Aural Contrast

Cinema of course has both sight and sound, and while a screenwriter cannot include contrasts in sound in his or her screenplay, sound cues, and contrasts therein, can be suggested by the screenwriter.

Important to remember is that contrast in auditory information—raising and lowering the volume of sounds and music—can likewise work in harmony with salient story points. A terrific example can be seen in *Toy Story* (1995): early in the film, during Andy's birthday party, there is much loud merriment, and the loud sounds of footsteps on the stairway and on the wooden floor. This is accompanied by loud music.

As soon as the children leave Andy's room, everything falls abruptly silent. This allows us to direct our attention to an important narrative element about to be revealed: what is the new toy that has taken Woody's place on the bed?

Examples of aural contrast in cinema are innumerable; a few examples here will suffice. In *Lawrence of Arabia,* Lawrence fails to rescue Daud from a quicksand in a howling wind storm, which has been

Figure 3.6 *Lawrence of Arabia* (1962) uses contrast in a great variety of ways, so it's not surprising to find contrast in its use of sound. Here, the film moves from a howling sandstorm to a nearly dead-silent march.

raging for more than two minutes of screen time. The film then cuts to a nearly silent image of Lawrence walking in front of his camel (see Figure 3.6). In *The Social Network*, loud club music is contrasted with classical music (see Figure 3.7).

Narrative Contrast: Tension and Release

In *Breaking Bad,* Walter White is driving his car along a highway, carrying a wad of illicit cash, gained from selling methamphetamine crystals. Suddenly, a police siren is heard, and, to his horror, a police car with flashing lights appears behind him, gaining fast. After a few agonizing moments in which he hides the wad of cash on the floor by his feet, he pulls over. *The police car whizzes past.*

Figure 3.7 A trifecta of contrast in two shots from *The Social Network* (2010): Dark/Light, Medium Shot/Long Shot, and loud dance club to serene countryside.

He (and the audience) realizes that the police car was chasing someone else. Both audience and character are relieved (see Figure 3.8).

This sequence is wholly unnecessary for the story: Walter winds up going where he has to go with the cash, and doing what he has to do. It could be cut out entirely, and the story would continue onward without any contradictions or confusions. But it's there, and good cinematic narrative is full of sequences like this.

The term for it is *preparation by contrast* (or, more technically, *priming*): giving clues to the audience to make it believe a given outcome is forthcoming, then delivering the opposite.

The reason skillful filmmakers employ preparation by contrast is not unlike why a roller-coaster ride has lots of ups and downs, and accelerations and decelerations, even though it deposits the rider in the same place that the ride started: to keep the rider engaged emotionally in the ride.

Figure 3.8 Walter is in deep trouble, then turns out not to be in so deep trouble after all. He got a scare, the audience got a scare, and as a reward to the screenwriter, everyone keeps on clicking the next episode. *Breaking Bad* (2008).

How Science Sees It, or, How to Avoid Narrative Exhaustion

Further along the visual pathway, our brain must prioritize the overwhelming amount of visual information our eyes detect. Two major selective processes are *perceptual salience* (bottom-up) and *momentary relevance* to the perceiver (top-down).[5]

Since the late 1990s, cognitive science has demonstrated that our emotional involvement or attachment to what we are watching or hearing *overrides executive control and captures attention*. That is, we can't help but be sucked in.

Emotional stimuli—whether visual or auditory (by music or language)—form a special case of highly salient perceptual processing, which demands attention and focuses audience's visual and comprehension processes on that stimuli. Such attention can be exhausting, and a filmmaker doesn't want his or her audience to be exhausted.

This is where contrast in tension comes into play: it is critical that a moment of high emotion be contrasted to a moment that is nonemotionally relevant. Screenwriters can time storyline information with highly emotional auditory or visual information for maximum effect on viewers more successfully if it is juxtaposed with relatively nonemotional sensory information.

Like worrying about a cop car, and then finding out such a worry is not justified.

Getting Emotional, or, How to Use the Word Valence in a Sentence about Screenwriting

Psychologists understand emotion in terms of *valences*, categorized as positive, negative, and neutral. Furthermore, they have learned that a positive valence, paired with a neutral one, creates a contrast that viewers will attend to more slowly, but *with sustained attention*. Meanwhile, a negative valence paired with a neutral one is a contrast that demands fast, *but short-lived* attentional processes.

---

5. E. Asutay. "Negative Emotion Provides Cues for Orienting Auditory Spatial Attention." *Frontiers in Psychology*, 6 (2015): 618. http://dx.doi.org/10.3389/fpsyg.2015.00618.

Figure 3.9 The appearance of the Sand People provide a brief interval of negative information, which in turn is followed by an extended period of positive information when Obi Wan rescues Luke and brings him to his home. According to psychologists, brief bursts of negative information are quickly absorbed by the viewer, but positive information can occupy more screen time because viewers attend to it with more sustained attention. *Star Wars* (1977).

For example, early in *Star Wars,* when Luke and C3P0 seek R2D2, who has run away, the audience is given a brief exposure (twenty seconds) to negative information (the Sand People are preparing to ambush). This is paired with a longer, neutral scene (45 seconds) in which Luke and C3P0 find R2D2, in danger but unaware of it and currently unthreatened. There follows another negative information scene (a little over a minute) in which Luke is attacked and then left unconscious, before Obi Wan shows up to make things right (see Figure 3.9).

The rescue—positive information—is now paired with a 6-minute-long scene in which Obi Wan provides Luke with shelter from danger and also informs him of information about his ancestry and, potentially,

The Science of Contrast 47

Figure 3.10 Valences at work: a rapid but brief burst of negative emotional information is ended by a longer scene of positive emotional information. *North by Northwest* (1959).

Figure 3.11 Valences at work. Part II: Negative emotional information is at play for about three minutes as the police pursue Roger on the train (top frame); this is followed by a slower-paced six-minute scene of positive emotional information, which in turn is ended with a burst of very negative emotional information—Roger is in danger and doesn't know it (bottom). *North by Northwest* (1959).

his destiny. The scene pairs positive and neutral information in various degrees; in all, it engages audience attention three times longer than the Sand People scenes.

Another example can be seen in *North by Northwest* (1959). Roger emerges from a phone booth at Grand Central Station and the audience is confronted with negative emotional information: he is in danger of being caught by the police. For the next three minutes, the negative/neutral valence is in operation, as Roger dodges the police and gets on a train (see Figure 3.10).

Here, he encounters Eve, who is very helpful to him, providing us with the positive/neutral valence that endures for more than six minutes, as the two get to know each other over lunch on the train.

This is interrupted by three minutes of the negative/neutral valence, during which the police arrive on the train and try to locate him (Figure 3.11). A six-minute lovemaking scene (very positive/neutral valence), which, in turn, is interrupted by the highly negative emotional information that in fact Roger, unbeknownst to him, is in mortal danger.

The Return of Top-Down

Contrast in pure light and darkness works the human mind over in a very elementary way; the emotions these situations convey are, to a large extent, learned. In childhood, low light, dark environments are associated with fear or negative information processing. Similarly, loud or disharmonic sounds are associated with danger—more negative information. Mastering the timing of onset and release from these perceptually induced negative emotions gives the filmmaker maximum control over audience attention.

It's worth noting that disharmonic music plays at the opening of *Double Indemnity* (1944) at the same time that we see a shadowy figure approach. The disharmonic music recurs throughout the film till justice is served in the final frames (see Figure 3.12).

Contrast in emotions and combinations of positive/neutral relative to negative/neutral, worked into your screenplay, your narrative story, are subliminally impacting your viewer's attention and comprehension. Lighting contrasts and audio cues are tools to direct your audience's sensory systems (ears and eyes) to what you want them to comprehend.

Figure 3.12 A menacing shadowy image, combined with loud, discordant music, marks the opening of *Double Indemnity* (1944), evoking a negative emotional response that relies on learned emotional signals. The discordant music, which recurs throughout, is finally resolved into concordance in the final scene.

What You Just Learned (or, Our Attempt to Load the above Information into Your Brain's Experience Structures; a Summary of Sorts)

- Contrast via light, sound, or action causes brain activity to adapt and synchronize firing; without it, viewers become bored as neuronal patterns cease processing. So tiny space ships being chased by huge space ships keep brain activity—well, active! *Narrative story line* as captured with eye trackers, shows that *saccades* and *fixations*—eye movements across and within scenes— are directed by what the viewer is comprehending of your story. Contrast in sound—loudness or silence—*aurally* causes similar changes in your audience –causing their brain activity patterns to snap out of idle and fully engage—literally, viewers become participants in your story.
- *Salient perceptual processes* (or, how to avoid narrative exhaustion) means *priming* or preparing viewers through clues to expect something and then delivering something entirely unexpected; the point being *tension must be contrasted with release*; a moment of high emotion needs to be contrasted to a moment that is nonemotionally relevant.
- The contrast of emotions, *valence,* as psychologists categorize our wide range of feelings into oversimplified positive versus negative versus neutral—is a powerful tool to *sustain attention* if the screenwriter contrasts the very negative/neutral and positive/neutral emotional information with those over-the-top moments of joy.

Screenwriting Explorations: Contrast and Atmosphere

Write three scenes. In the first one, a character arrives at an unfamiliar location and encounters another person unexpectedly. In the second scene, some time later, that same character arrives at the same location and is expecting to meet that other person. In the third scene, later still, the same character arrives at the same location, only this time the other character is no longer there. Use no dialogue: sight and sound only. When writing these, give attention to how contrasting atmospheres can enhance the effect of the scenes on the audience. What lighting conditions (time of day, weather, etc.) are best employed in the scenes? How can variations in atmosphere, lighting, be employed to better tell the story you have told?

Perceptual Prompts—Simultaneous Contrast

Our rods are responsive to edges—that visual information that we are approaching a boundary is, of course, survival based. The light is reflected differently by the top of an object relative to the object's sides or the surface beneath. Or is it? Measurements of reflected light can be exactly the same from two objects, but if backgrounds reflect different amounts of light we perceive differences in the objects that do not exist.

Or try this shadow casting yourself: Use a bright desk lamp so that it shines directly on a white piece of paper. Then cast a shadow by holding a card or book in between the light and the paper. The gray bands of the shadow appear to be darker closer to the edge of the intruding object and grow lighter the further the shadow extends away from the edge. This seeing borders (Mach bands) is unrelated to physical changes in bottom-up information. Nothing changed in your desk lamp or the piece of paper—your brain creates contrast to keep you from missing borders!

Figure 3.13 Perceptual prompt—simultaneous contrast.

Chapter 4

THE SCIENCE OF EXPOSITION, OR, WHAT'S WRONG WITH AN INFORMATION DUMP?

In order to become emotionally involved in a film, the audience needs to know the answers to the questions of who, what, when, where, and under what conditions the picture will take place. This information is called *exposition*. If we don't know the answers to those questions, we are only observers watching things happen, unable to connect emotionally with any of the characters, and will likely tune out (see Chapter 2). If we know the answers, we have the capacity to experience hope and fear about what is happening, that is, we are inclined to stay tuned in, get to be blown away emotionally, and tell our friends they *have* to see the movie.

The tricky part of writing exposition is that it tends to be concentrated in the early part of the film, which is precisely when the writer/filmmaker needs to hook the audience and pull it along for the ride. Accordingly, many screenwriting manuals have issued warnings or careful instructions about how to handle it.

David Howard tells us that "exposition should be used sparingly ... overuse of exposition quickly becomes tedious to the audience."[1]

How to handle it? Blake Snyder gives this advice: "Give me the facts, ma'am, just the facts, but please do it in a way that won't put me to sleep. Thus, exposition—like annoying plot details, heist plans, and backstories—can't be just laid out, it must be entertainingly told by crafty screenwriters. To 'bury' said exposition is to deal with it in a way that is not deadly dull. The masters of the craft make these irritating facts and figures go down as easily as a spoonful of Maypo."[2]

---

1. David Howard and Edward Mabley, *The Tools of Screenwriting* (New York: St. Martin's Griffin, 1995), p. 60.
2. Blake Snyder, *Save the Cat* (Studio City, CA: Michael Wiese Productions, 2005), p. 185.

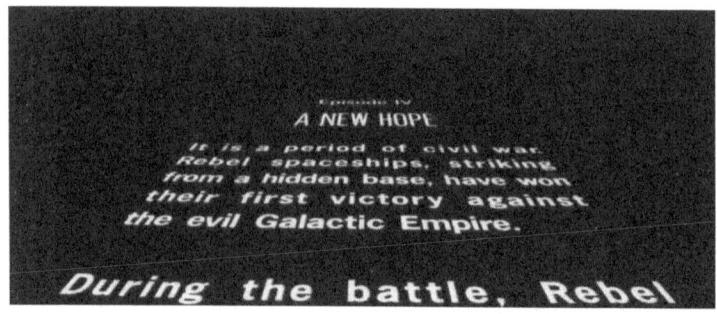

Figure 4.1 The "Mother of All Information Dumps": the opening title crawl from *Star Wars* (1977). If you didn't bring a notebook to the movie theater, you probably didn't remember a lot of this information. However, that's okay, because it was really just an *homage* to 1930s' serials (see Figure 4.2) and the film will soon enough catch you up on everything you need to know. The human mind is ill-equipped to handle information dumps.

Figure 4.2 The "Grandmother of All Information Dumps": the opening title crawl from an episode of *Flash Gordon* (1936).

Unfortunately, Snyder leaves several questions unanswered, such as: how do "crafty screenwriters" do it? Or, more specifically, how does one become a master of the craft? And, by the way, what is *Maypo*?

Robert McKee is a bit more helpful: "You do not keep the audience's interest by giving it information, but by withholding information, except that which is absolutely necessary for comprehension ... Pace exposition ... save the best for last ... create the desire to know by arousing curiosity ... with a hunger for information, even the most complicated set of dramatized facts will pass smoothly into understanding."[3]

Constructivist Psychology to the Rescue

Fortunately, science can fill in a few gaps left by the above-cited authorities; in particular, how our brain seeks patterns, how our brain wants to use as little energy as possible, and how your crafting of clever exposition can rely on schemas. In short, you'll learn how to unlock the mysteries of exposition and learn how to be like the "masters," craftily handling it a certain way.

We've already seen (in Chapter 1) how humans perceive the world in terms of clues, rather than complete information. There is simply far too much going on in the world for our merely mortal sense organs—and brain—to process absolutely everything. So we take shortcuts by making assumptions about what we perceive based on previous experience—top-down versus bottom-up processing.

To use more technical language, we experience two directions of information flow: first, all stimulus coming in from the real world (light, sound, touch, etc.) is transduced from that form of energy into the electrochemical neural impulses, which proceed in an orderly fashion throughout our brain; this is the bottom-up information of sensation and perception; no thinking or feeling involved. But once this electrochemical information arrives in our cortical (thinking brain areas), it has passed through our more primitive, subcortical emotion centers, and our individual life experiences, preferences and opinions have been added. This is our top-down information—who we are decides how we are going to respond.

As Chapter 1 explained, this could either get you to climb a tree quickly, or engage in play with your dog. Collectively, these life experiences organize certain things we know about various life concepts into shortcuts called schemas. Human experience is largely shared, that

---

3. Robert McKee, *Story: Substance, Structure, Style, and the Principles of Screenwriting* (New York: HarperCollins, 1997), pp. 335–7.

is, most people have experienced a birthday party, a car, train, plane ride, or a ballgame, or simply going to movie. We have general knowledge that a ballgame will likely include two teams, uniforms, bleachers, spectators, and maybe beer. These associated bits of information clump together as our "ballgame" schema, and so we anticipate seeing or hearing these associations when planning to attend a ballgame. We rely on our schemas so predictably that our heads, eyes, even our steps or reaching grasp are ready to respond to what transpires in the game. Schemas direct our exploration of the environment. How can the crafty screenwriter use schemas to smuggle in the who, what, where information? Trust that your audience is already applying their schemas for going to a movie. This is imagination run real, so people know the basics.

The key is these are what are called *nonvolitional* processes—that is, we can't help ourselves. Our brains, when we're conscious, are in a constant state of taking in data and processing it in this way: taking in cues and putting them together into a more complete picture or understanding. How can a screenwriter exploit this fact? Let's examine two who did.

Ninotchka (1939)

In order to understand the action in this classic (screenplay by Charles Brackett, Billy Wilder, and Walter Reisch; story by Melchior Lengyel; directed by Ernst Lubitsch) you need to know that three Russian envoys, Buljanoff, Iranoff, and Kopalski, have arrived in Paris to sell jewels that were confiscated from Russian Princess Swana during the Bolshevik Revolution of 1917. One option is for the storytellers to do a title crawl and simply dump all this information before the audience, and get on with the story.

Instead, they began with a shot of a suspicious-looking man entering a fancy hotel and looking around furtively, followed by another, then another; none of them is interested in help from the hotel manager (see Figure 4.3).

The opening is not information rich; however, it contains some cues and clues that play on our propensity to create understanding out of incomplete information. We will at first recognize a fancy hotel—this is something within the experience of most viewers. Then, an

Figure 4.3 The opening shots of *Ninotchka* (1939). The storytellers exploited the audience's irresistible reflex of constructing hypotheses out of clues in order to get us hooked.

anomaly: some shabbily dressed individuals who exhibit behavior we consider suspicious, again based on previous experiences.

It is only after our brains have begun to process this intriguing information—and thus made ready for more information—that we get some answers: the individuals are not thieves, but rather from Moscow on some sort of a mission. However, this new information isn't simply dropped all at once; instead, dialogue occurs, which, again, gives the audience clues, rather than complete information. The third of the three, Kopalski, emerges from the hotel and talks to the other two:

> **KOPALSKI:** Comrades, why should we lie to each other? It's wonderful.
> **IRANOFF:** Let's be honest. Have we anything like it in Russia?
> **ALL THREE** (agreeing with him): No, no, no.
> **IRANOFF:** Can you imagine what the beds would be in a hotel like that?
> **KOPALSKI:** They tell me when you ring once the valet comes in; when you ring twice you get the waiter; and do you know what happens when you ring three times? A maid comes in— a French maid.
> **IRANOFF** *(with a gleam in his eye):* Comrades, if we ring nine times ... let's go in.
> **BULJANOFF** *(stopping him):* Just a minute—just a minute—I have nothing against the idea but I still say let's go back to the Hotel Terminus. Moscow made our reservations there, we are on an official mission, and we have no right to change the orders of our superior.
> **IRANOFF:** Where is your courage, Comrade Buljanoff?
> **KOPALSKI:** Are you the Buljanoff who fought on the barricades? And now you are afraid to take a room with a bath?
> **BULJANOFF** *(stepping back into the taxi):* I don't want to go to Siberia.
> *(Iranoff and Kopalski follow him reluctantly).*
> **IRANOFF:** I don't want to go to the Hotel Terminus.
> **KOPALSKI:** If Lenin were alive he would say, "Buljanoff, Comrade, for once in your life you're in Paris. Don't be a fool. Go in there and ring three times."
> **IRANOFF:** He wouldn't say that. What he would say is "Buljanoff, you can't afford to live in a cheap hotel. Doesn't

the prestige of the Bolsheviks mean anything to you? Do you want to live in a hotel where you press for the hot water and cold water comes and when you press for the cold water nothing comes out at all? Phooey, Buljanoff!"

BULJANOFF *(weakening)*: I still say our place is with the common people, but who am I to contradict Lenin? Let's go in.

Instead of information, we witness a conversation—or more specifically, an argument. We are not involved in the argument, and nothing in it is directed at us; we merely overhear it. Everything we learn is by inference. The use of the word *comrade* lets us know—anyway those of us acquainted with some history—that these are Russian communists, the nationality confirmed by the type of dress, the references to Russia, and the accents. We further learn about their relative power position—under the thumb of Moscow and afraid of its power—as well as their past as participants in the revolution. We also get a sense of their reasoning process.

During the next few scenes, we continue to overhear their conversations—with the hotel manager, and later on the phone with a jeweler—and by these clues we are able to construct an understanding of the information noted before. Our schema for hotels and room service fill in what's not directly stated in conversation. Our schema for *comrade*—partners or coworkers—prepares us to anticipate a hierarchy relationship with the details of who's who and what are the rules in this scenario, acting as curiosity lures, to keep us engaged while the exposition is expertly delivered.

The film accomplishes this in just under five minutes. True enough, a simple title crawl could do it faster, but because the simple listing of pure information does *not* exploit our natural perceptual processes, it's unlikely we would remember any of it for long. The experience would not be unlike that of following a recipe—few of us can follow a recipe once—with its lists of ingredients and step-by-step instructions—without having to go back and reread it frequently.

Our brains just don't absorb information dumps well.

A more recent example can be seen in *Silver Linings Playbook* (2012). In order to understand the action in this film, it is necessary to know that Pat (Bradley Cooper) caught his wife cheating on him with a history teacher from the high school where they both worked, went berserk and nearly murdered him. He's been in a mental facility for eight months and hopes to regain his place again.

Figure 4.4 The opening shot of *Silver Linings Playbook* (2012). Pat's back is turned to us and he's mumbling about football Sundays. Thus begins the puzzle that triggers the mind's attention to details that help us understand the story.

Again, these facts could be dumped on the audience in the screen crawl, but, like *Ninotchka*, this film begins with a puzzle. True enough, there is a bit of "pure information": the white title "Karel Psychiatric Facility, Baltimore" on black. Already, though, a puzzle emerges: a disembodied voice talking about Sunday football. The first image is of a man with his back to us, alone in a small room, apparently talking to himself (see Figure 4.5). In rapid succession, we see his environs, learn his name (Pat), and overhear an argument between his mother and an administrator, then overhear a conversation about his plans for the future, before winding up at his house, where more argument ensues, with his father Pat Sr. It isn't until fourteen minutes into the picture that we learn, from a conversation with a psychiatrist, about the episode in which he nearly killed the history teacher.

That fourteen minutes is well spent because by giving the audience cues and clues, the mind's irresistible tendency to construct understanding from these cues and clues more firmly lodges that information in us: we're not going to easily forget it.

Can I Become a Crafty Screenwriter Too?

Thanks to constructivist psychology, the answer is clearly *yes*. The masters have certainly delivered exposition "sparingly" (Howard's advice), informed by the creation of curiosity by the audience, per McKee. Beyond these, though, is a systematic way of thinking about exposition. The writer/filmmaker is actually in charge of how the audience puts the clues together. As noted screenwriting professor Frank Daniel exhorted his students, "Your job is to make the audience the smartest people in the world. Let them feel they are very good observers of detail. They will always be therefore trying to second-guess you as to what is coming next."[4] He further noted that the writer is actually playing a game with the audience in this respect.

One common mistake that novice (and not-so-novice) writers make is to begin their scripts with story immediately. In fact, the best way to begin is with a *puzzle*. Throw out puzzling clues and cues to the audience, designed to create a certain understanding of the world they are encountering on film, and let the nonvolitional unconscious processes of constructivist psychology do the rest. This kind of approach will make the information go down at least as smoothly as fine sushi.

The Science behind Otherworldly Worlds

A side issue one might consider with respect to exposition: how can it work in a film that is literally out of this world? After all, the "top-down" perceptual processes that drive comprehension are based on our experiences, and yet we have little difficulty understanding *Star Wars,* even though only about five hundred mortals have ever been in outer space—hardly enough to fuel its $786 million in worldwide box office sales.

As discussed in Chapter 1, one explanation is the nature of audience intention when entering a movie theater. Movie watchers have removed themselves from "reality" and their intention (besides entertainment) is to engage in the *illusion* of reality.[5] Still, one must create that illusion with sufficient familiarity that viewers can construct connections from their schemas of travel, to the star voyagers. Importantly, there is no attempt in *Star Wars* to lure the audience into their own acquaintance with space travel. So how did viewers make such a connection to something out of this world (and not in their schemas)?

    4. Frank Daniel, *Workshop Lecture* (New York: Columbia University, September 1979).
    5. N. Carroll and W. P. Seeley, "Cognitivism, Psychology, and Neuroscience: Movies as Attentional Engines," in *Psychocinematics: Exploring Cognition at the Movies,* ed. Arthur P. Shimamura, pp. 53–75 (Oxford: Oxford University Press, 2013).

Figure 4.5 Ever flown one of these? If not, join the club. Audiences cannot draw on past experience in space ships to understand *Star Wars*, but the filmmakers could rely on analogous, earth-bound experiences like driving a car. The result was millions of nonastronauts paying cash to see the film. *Star Wars* (1977).

Let's back up, reconsider the top-down information involved in watching the opening space ship battle. Our real experience with vehicles is vast and can be simplified something like this: vehicles move faster than people can, contain people, are controlled and directed by people, usually with the intention of transporting said people from point A to point B. And all of that top-down experience is consistent with watching space ships engage in high-speed maneuvers, even though it is unlikely anyone in the audience has actually flown a space ship. So our brains use what we have to explain, in logical detail, what we haven't experienced. It is this process, this binding of what's on the screen, with real-world experience, that screenwriters may craftily employ in exposition.

A writer/filmmaker has to carefully include enough "reality" so that the illusion carries cognitive grip. Schemas, our existing understanding of movies and various plots or scenes, will go to great lengths to sustain comprehension. Neurons, individual cells, can only fire in a sequential, linear manner. Once fired, that neuron must regroup, as it were, before further incoming information can generate another response. So scenes and sequences carefully balanced with sufficient content of nonillusory objects or actions engage the viewer's schemas. Their own life experiences connect them to your movie and allow the writer/filmmaker to sustain or direct viewer's attention to cues, which the viewer will grasp even though they contain elements beyond their experience—for example, spaceships.[6]

6. Carroll and Seeley "Cognitivism, Psychology, and Neuroscience."

What You Just Learned (or, Our Attempt to Load the Above Information into Your Brain's Experience Structures, a Summary of Sorts)

A time-consuming, tediously boring *information dump* can overwhelm your reader or viewer almost immediately, causing loss of interest in your screenplay. Advice manuals tend to agree—getting the background facts established early is critical to reader comprehension, but saying more with less is key to keeping audience's attention. Information that is withheld or supplied teasingly will keep readers guessing; or as *constructionist psychology* suggests, allows your audience to rely on their *schemas*. Providing true information in clues, instead of stating the facts, provokes audience participation—we want to verify our schematic assumptions—are we right? It is thus best to begin your screenplay with a *puzzle, not a story*.

Screenwriting Explorations: Exposition as a Game with the Audience

Write a scene taking place in a restaurant or another location in which one character overhears the conversation of two (or more) other characters. Write the scene strictly from the listener's point of view—we do not see the people talking. Write the dialogue in such a way as to present clues to the listener (and reader) that can then be put together to create an impression of what the others are talking about. By the end of the scene, the character who is listening becomes motivated (for whatever reason you choose, presumably based on what he or she has concluded about the conversation) to confront those having the conversation. Come up with a twist for the ending.

This is an exercise in giving clues to the audience—in this case, lines of dialogue—from which we can infer details about the people talking—who they are, what their relationships are, what they are seeking. That is, *exposition*. However, with the twist, it also demonstrates how we can construct the wrong impression based on clues alone: the clues can lend the impression of one scenario taking place, but upon discovering the reality of the situation, the character [and audience] can see how the clues could be added together to construct an alternative scenario).

Perceptual Prompts—Where Is That Noise Coming from?

Our auditory system provides both what and where information from sounds (which is the result of changes in air pressure around us). Scientists measure how we locate sound by coordinates of azimuth (left-to-right) and elevation (up-down). Try this on a few different people and see if your data confirm—most of us are pretty accurate at locating where a noise is coming from if it's in front of us. If the sound is behind us, either coordinate is less helpful.

Tell your helper you are going to jangle your keys from various positions and with their eyes closed they should indicate where the sound is coming from. Have a chair close by on both sides and in front and behind your helper. Then jangle from multiple positions, left, right, above, below their head. Note the accuracy differences when you are in front versus behind your helper. Do this with several different people as hearing ability varies widely for many reasons, but soon enough you'll have a new appreciation for why we have audiences face the screen!

Chapter 5

THE SCIENCE OF CAUSE AND EFFECT, OR, DID THE PACKERS REALLY LOSE BECAUSE I DIDN'T WEAR MY CHEESEHEAD HAT?

A long time ago, the Greek philosopher Aristotle (384–322 BCE) made a simple and eloquent argument about cause and effect in drama:

> A whole is that which has a beginning, a middle, and an end. A beginning is that which does not itself follow anything by causal necessity, but after which something naturally is or comes to be. An end, on the contrary, is that which itself naturally follows some other thing, either by necessity, or as a rule, but has nothing following it. A middle is that which follows something as some other thing follows it.[1]

Gustav Freytag put it this way:

> The action must move forward with uniform consistency [which] is produced by representing an event which follows another, as an effect of which that other is the evident cause ... This binding together of incidents by the free creation of a causative connection, is the distinguishing characteristic of this species of art.[2]

The notion of cause and effect is so deeply embedded in our common sense that it may escape a filmmaker's notice to see how it can be exploited in maintaining audience (and reader) involvement in a story. Yet, the notion of a character with a drive toward a goal—a basic pattern stressed in many manuals of screenwriting—implies cause and effect—the main action of a character seeking a goal is the effect of the cause of

---

1. Aristotle, *The Poetics*. Trans. S. H. Butcher (New York: Macmillan, 1902), p. 31.
2. Gustav Freytag, *Technique of the Drama: An Exposition of Dramatic Composition and Art*. Trans. E. J. MacEwan (Chicago, IL: Scott, Foresman, 1900), p. 29.

that character's desire for that goal.[3] Pat's desire to reunite with his wife is the cause that leads to all the unfolding events, actions, and counter-actions in *Silver Linings Playbook* (2012).

Mark's socially awkward manner is the cause that leads to the many and various effects—actions and reactions—that provide the content for *The Social Network* (2010). It's a complex, richly written film with many characters and complications, and much of it is told out of order. Nonetheless, the viewer can trace an unbroken chain of causes and effects accounting for everything that happens: Mark insults Erica, which causes her to reject him, which wounds him sufficiently to lash out by hacking into the Harvard computer system, which brings him notoriety on campus, which brings him to the attention of the Winkelvoss twins—upper classmen—who employ him to work for them. This contact—depending on how you view it—was either a dead end for Mark or it inspired him to create Facebook. Either way, he is inspired by the idea, which leads him to put everything aside to do the necessary programming, recruit others to help him, and bring in his friend Eduardo for financial backing. It also brings Mark and Eduardo the attention of women, who befriend them. The launching of the site causes a negative reaction from the Winkelvoss twins, who feel cheated, and who thus pursue legal action against Mark; it also brings their project to the attention of Sean Parker, who leads Mark to huge financial rewards but causes a break between him and Eduardo, causing the latter to join in suing him. The effect of the final cause—the two lawsuits filed against Mark—are left to dangle into the future, though an effect is hinted at by a young attorney at the end, who tells Mark he will settle.

If a screenplay's pages follow one another in a cause-and-effect pattern, reader comprehension and engagement is much easier to accomplish; indeed, a screenplay with scenes that follow one another *without* a clear causal connection can be difficult for a reader to keep track of. Ensemble films, and those which may begin with several parallel lines of action, are particularly challenging in this regard, and need

---

3. David Bordwell, in *Narration in the Fiction Film*, notes, "One researcher found that comprehension and memory are best when the story conformed to the drive-to-a-goal pattern. When the goal was stated at the end of the tale, comprehension and recall were significantly poorer, but still not so poor as when the goal of the action was never stated" (p. 35).

to be handled carefully so as to maintain audience focus. Note that in *The Social Network*, it would have been possible to begin the film with Mark and his world, then introduce a parallel action involving the Winkelvoss twins, and then also introduce Sean Parker, and portray all three lines of action in parallel until they intersect. The storytellers instead chose to introduce these additional characters only when the chain of cause and effect brought them in contact with Mark's story line.

The opening of *Bullets over Broadway* (1994) demonstrates a technique of how to maintain audience interest when scenes do *not* follow each other by cause-and-effect pattern. The premise of the movie involves a playwright, David, who needs to raise money to get his play produced. His producer, Julian, manages to make a deal for the money with a notorious gangster, Nick, on the condition that Nick's girlfriend Olive be given a role in the play. It would have been possible to develop this story in a manner similar to the approach used in *The Social Network*—David pursues his objective—cause-and-effect sequencing—and in the process he meets Valenti, who gives him funding, much like the Peter Thiel character does in *The Social Network*. Instead, writers Woody Allen and Douglas McGrath chose to open the film with two threads that are unrelated causally—we meet David and Julian and learn about David's predicament, then we immediately meet Valenti and Olive, and learn about her dreams of Broadway stardom. In order to smooth over the lack of a cause-and-effect relationship between these threads, a *dialogue hook* is employed. At the end of the opening scene, Julian warns David: "That's the real world out there. And it's a lot rougher place than you think." The film immediately cuts to a group of mobsters gunning down victims in a dark alley. Although there is no causal connection between the scenes, there is a common *motif*: violence. This can serve to give the scenes the sense of a causal connection even when there isn't one.

The Shop around the Corner (1940) has a slightly different challenge and uses a different solution. This is predominantly an ensemble piece with various subplots. The narrative thus meanders a bit at the beginning as the various characters who work in a shop are introduced. To forestall the problem of an audience's meandering attention (and combat the expectation audiences may have—that almost all movies begin with a single line of action involving cause and effect), the filmmakers opted to put what amounts to a disclaimer in the opening shot of the picture (see Figure 5.1).

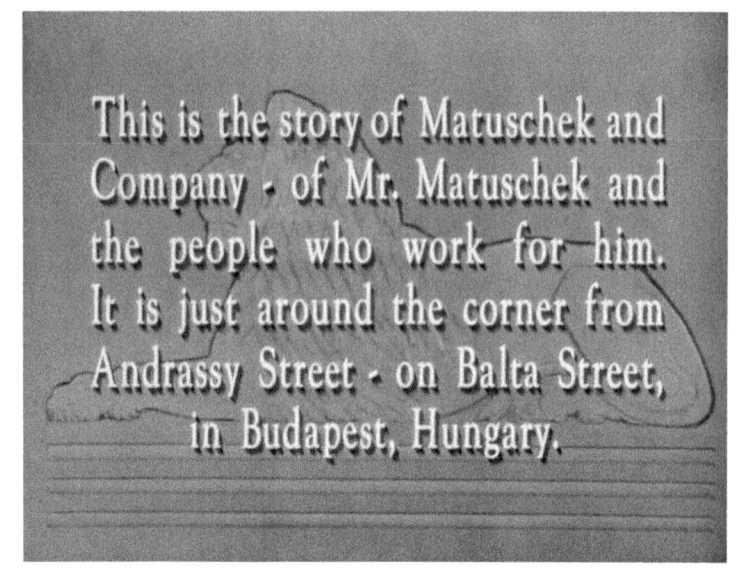

> This is the story of Matuschek and Company - of Mr. Matuschek and the people who work for him. It is just around the corner from Andrassy Street - on Balta Street, in Budapest, Hungary.

Figure 5.1 Director Ernst Lubistch added this title card to the opening of *The Shop around the Corner* (1940). It was not in the original script; its presence serves to disarm audience confusion that might result from a lack of cause-and-effect sequencing in the first portion of the film.

The Science

Along with deep subcortical connections to our emotion centers, our brains also uniquely evolved connections, which support causal reasoning. Humans, like no other species, insist on cause-and-effect explanations. If a dog, for example, comes upon some food, he or she will simply devour it, and not question where it came from. Humans, in the same situation, will try to figure out what *caused* the food to be there. This is obviously a great advantage from a survival point of view. If we can figure out the cause, we may be able to get more. Greater nutrition means a higher likelihood of successful reproduction.

Human understanding of cause-and-effect relationships begins with language. From birth, children pursue mastery of their native language every waking moment. They learn early on that certain sounds they make cause certain responses from their parents or other caregivers.

Such cause-and-effect stimuli proceed through our emotion centers to our frontal reasoning areas (see Figure 2.3).

Through repetition, our brains build positive feedback pathways that traverse directly through our language centers. We thus feel good when we understand the connection between our words and the actions of others, and vice versa. Communication through language thus becomes the best activator of our "feel good" system, because our brains have cleverly ensured we would seek to understand by linking endorphin rewards with language comprehension.

From this initial understanding of cause and effect, our comprehension of the world spreads. Our brains function from a primal perspective—survival first. Thus, physical drives of hunger, thirst, shelter, sex, and avoidance of pain are the basic causes that all of us address daily; if rather benignly for those of us so situated as to be well fed and nestled in homes with loving family. Our conscious daily efforts, whether bushman or playwright, to seek food and shelter, are the cause—and the effect is we beat the bushes or struggle through a manuscript into the night: whatever it takes to put bread on the table.

This physical level of cause has predictable effects and carries over to the physical world we live in. Physical cause-and-effect relations are learned readily and early and remain true almost under all conditions. So we expect water to extinguish fire, we understand objects fall but don't float in mid-air ordinarily, and even, in most civilized countries, that aspirin relieves pain. This physical knowledge of cause and effect has been described as the basic level of comprehension and decades of language comprehension research indicate we draw inferences from physical cause and effect even under conditions of distraction or stress.[4] We thus understand and experience the world through the prism of cause and effect—and narrative comprehension is not far behind. A cause-and-effect relationship is, in essence, a narrative, a series of events unfolding in time. Soon this understanding of cause and effect spreads to most of our experience of the world, including understanding the *intentions* of people we encounter as a cause of their behavior, and intervals of time and distances in space, as cause and effect on events that unfold.

4. A. Graesser, M. Singer, and T. Trabasso, "Constructing Inferences during Narrative Text Comprehension." *Psychological Review*, 101 (1994): 371–95.

Thus, screenplays and films that evince cause-and-effect sequencing fit neatly into our disposition to find such patterns in life, and readers/audiences will rely on these reality-driven mental processes to follow the unfolding story.[5]

Rewind: But *The Social Network Is Told Out of Order*

Many screenplays unfold in a nonlinear way—*Citizen Kane, Double Indemnity, Memento,* and *(500) Days of Summer* come to mind, along with *The Social Network*, which alternates between the overall narrative line with its cause-and-effect sequencing, and two legal depositions that occurred subsequent to the main action. The question is: why, if humans are so predisposed to follow a cause-and-effect pattern, do these films work?

The answer lies in that very propensity to see the world in terms of cause and effect—it's how we interpret the world—and in our propensity to seek clues to create understanding. Remember Jaak Panksepp from Chapter 2?

Behavioral research has demonstrated that readers encode, store, and build mental representations of narrative texts. Real-world aspects of these mental representations—causal relations, intentions of characters, even spatial and temporal indices—can be tested in forms of accuracy to comprehension questions, or memory recall or even reading times for a sentence or script. If a reader must go back and reread a sentence—or a producer has to reread a scene—this longer time reading implies more difficulty in comprehending. Thus, faster reading times indicate faster comprehension of the material being read. Such data suggest that manipulations which vary reality indices (e.g., time—a moment later vs. a day later vs. the following week) influence comprehension such that readers are now expecting different spatial settings, changes in intentions, and so forth.[6] Movie audiences will also rely on these reality-driven mental processes to follow the unfolding story. Essentially, audiences will use the clues presented (a deposition that seems out of order) to *construct* a linear cause-and-effect narrative even if there isn't one in the film or screenplay. The key to such a

---

5. D. N. Rapp and R. Gerrig, "Readers' Reality-Driven and Plot-Driven Analyses in Narrative Comprehension." *Memory & Cognition*, 20 (5) (2002): 779–88.

6. Rapp and Gerrig, "Readers' Reality-Driven and Plot-Driven Analyses in Narrative Comprehension," 779–88.

Figure 5.2 Two deposition scenes are fractured and then interspersed throughout the sequential narrative of *The Social Network* (2010), presenting the viewer with an out-of-order film that challenges a cause-and-effect understanding. The human brain is up to the task, though: we will tend to construct a cause-and-effect understanding of the material based on clues within it.

structure is to be sure to hook the audience and maintain its attention by various means (many described in this book) until enough clues about the cause-and-effect sequencing are conveyed. In the case of *The Social Network*, the film follows a strict cause-and-effect sequencing for its first sixteen minutes—enough time to get the audience oriented.

Causes with a Delayed Effect

Gulino (2004) describes a *dangling cause* as a "tool" that screenwriters can use to sustain audience interest. It's a "cause" in the form of a character making an expression of intent, a warning or threat, expression of hope or fear or a prediction. These will keep the audience in anticipation for the resulting effect. That is, the cause "dangles" in the mind of the audience for a while before the effect is witnessed.

In the major study of American cinematic storytelling, *The Classical Hollywood Cinema: Film Style & Mode of Production to 1960*, by David Bordwell, Kristin Thompson, and Janet Staiger (1985), it's described as the "most basic cause of temporal and causal clarity."[7] It was anticipated by Frank Daniel, as noted in David Howard's *The Tools of Screenwriting*

---

7. David Bordwell, Kristin Thompson, and Janet Staiger, *The Classical Hollywood Cinema: Film Style & Mode of Production to 1960* (New York: Columbia University Press, 1985), pp. 19–20.

Figure 5.3 A rare visual *dangling cause*, from *Toy Story* (1995). Most dangling causes are delivered verbally.

where Howard uses the phrase *Elements of the Future* to describe a similar idea: "predictions, omens, daydreams and assurances" that serve to "encourage the audience to look to the future of the story."[8]

Successful films usually have these in abundance. A substantial number of lines uttered by Pat in the first part of *Silver Linings Playbook* consist of dangling causes: "I want to read the entire high school English syllabus. Mom, it's a good thing. I'm remaking myself." And, "What am I doing? I'm getting in shape. I'm getting trim. I'm getting really fit for Nikki. Gonna read Nikki's teaching syllabus and get my old job back." And, "You know what I'm doing to do? I'm going to take all this negativity and I'm going to use it as fuel and I'm going to find a silver lining, that's what I'm going to do."

In *The Social Network*, Divya tells Mark: "I can't wait to stand over your shoulder and watch you write us a check." In *Lawrence of Arabia* (1962), Lawrence tells Sherif Ali: "Aqaba is that way. It is only a matter of going." Sefton tells his fellow prisoners in *Stalag 17* (1954), "There are two guys in this barracks that know I didn't do it. Me, and the guy who *did* do it ... and he'd better watch out, the guy who left me holding the stick. Because if there are going to be any throats cut ..." In *The Shop Around the Corner* (1940), Kralik tells Pirovitch, "this girl thinks I'm

---

8. David Howard and Edward Mabley, *The Tools of Screenwriting* (New York: St. Martin's Griffin, 1995), p. 75.

the most wonderful person in the world, and there's a chance she may be disappointed." *Toy Story* (1995) features a rarity: a visual dangling cause. Sketch draws a picture of a hanging noose, and Hamm aims it at Woody (see Figure 5.4).

These dangling causes are motivated by what is happening in the various scenes, but they are aimed squarely at the audience to keep them in a state of anticipating the future of the narrative.

The Science

Expressions of intent are described by psychologists as *motives* and motives require a more complex understanding of cause and effect. While physical cause-and-effect sequences (water puts out fire) are readily comprehended, motives, or plans, require the understanding that an expression of intent suggests that a goal has been set and a sequence of actions toward that goal would support comprehension. This is not as clear-cut as physical cause and effect, because any number of actions may lead to goal achievement. This means the reader or viewer must evaluate each move the character initiates in terms of moving toward the goal or moving away from the goal—this cognitive exercise can keep an audience engaged, but is exhausting. Neuroimaging studies have shown that when we are reading along and events or actions are consistent with aforementioned intents or goals, our brains produce a relatively smooth electrical pattern. When we come across an inconsistent action, a sharp negative spike (N400) disrupts the comprehension process, which scientists claim is our brain's way of informing us something is off—the goal state is in jeopardy. For example, the goal state in *Silver Linings Playbook* is for Pat to improve himself so that he may win back his estranged wife. Consistent electrical patterns in viewer's brains follow his plans to read and exercise. But, when Pat runs into conflict by the principle's response, *wham!* N400 spikes! Viewers see this as trouble for Pat's goal state.

In reading, this causes our eyes to backtrack, read again; we search for the cause of moving away from the intention or goal state. If the inconsistency is not resolved by rereading, we forge ahead, seeking explanation. When a movie abruptly discards a character's intention, viewers are in the discomfort of N400 spikes. If the film is being watched in a theater, there is no "rewind" to fill in the error, so the viewer sustains the inconsistent diversion, in anticipation of explanation. Even if the film or TV show is viewed at home (or being read in script form), to stop and rewind it is to violate the viewer's immersion in the cinematic experience, diminishing its impact.

This cognitive commitment involves an interplay between the structural aspects of the audience's comprehension (what is the story, where is the setting, who are the characters) and the associative components of emotions a viewer is experiencing (See Chapter 1, CAM-WN). This means readers or viewers are basically juggling how they feel about the character's setback, seeking to predict or anticipate alternative actions the character may attempt to realign with original goals, and updating their comprehension of the unfolding narrative.

The audience is building a "working narrative" as the story unfolds, this is the "cloud" from Cohen's CAM model. Our brains fire along smoothly until an inconsistent action or event derails a goal; forcing the audience to reexamine, focus on bottom-up auditory or visual information, to make sense or reestablish comprehension. Cohen calls this the *working narrative*, which is informed by dialogue, visual settings and actions, and auditory music or sound effects. As the "realities" of the movie assemble in the viewer's working narrative, everything is subjected to personal preferences, expectations, and general knowledge of the viewer's life, including social norms (see Chapter 1--The CAM-WN model).

An interesting combination of filmic tools can be seen with the specifics of background music. Here, the audience emotionally responds to the swell of well-orchestrated strings while the characters embrace—a congruent emotion for the visual scene. Yet, the audience somehow knows that the characters do not hear the music—that the 'real' world of the characters is distinct from the associated emotional surge that the music provides to the audience. An excellent example of reversing the emotional connection is demonstrated in *Blazing Saddles* (1974), when the sheriff rides across the desert to the background big band *April in Paris*, which is consistent with the storyline and the audience assumes is associated (i.e., the sheriff does not hear the big band) until the sheriff unexpectedly comes across Count Basie and band playing live in the desert. Knowing that movie watchers expect music—unless directly part of the scene—to be second-order information, intended to increase emotional responses, can lead successfully to overcome N400 coherence breaks.[9] (See Chapter 1 for examples of *schema violations*.)

9. Cohen, A. J., "Film Music and the Unfolding Narrative." In *Language, Music and the Brain*, edited by M. A. Arbib, pp. 173–201 (Cambridge, MA: MIT Press, 2013).

Time lapses, leaps forward or back across time, can be visually signaled and rapidly comprehended by experienced viewers. Yet, movies that fail to consider the audience's mental representation—that if time changes, then spatial relations and progress on character's intentions are expected to change as well—may lose an audience in a flood of N400 spikes of confusion. Look again at Cohen's model; the bottom-up sensory information channels all combine with structure and meaning to contribute to the viewer's ongoing working narrative. And working narratives are fed into by the viewer's top-down knowledge of life, resulting in expectations that if time has changed, so have people, places, and situations.

The relevance to screenwriter's use of brain processes is to accept that viewers are seeking information about the characters from a subconscious perspective. Our human nature is to seek a causal explanation but it is not innate, as our real-world experience plays a critical role in forming our emotional responses and our expectations. It is important for screenwriters to understand that an audience's perspective to find causal explanations is why the audience begins to form the so-called hook questions: "Is she going to get out of this mess? Is she going to …" In other words, the flow of bottom-up visual and auditory information is literally smothered in emotions of which a viewer may have no awareness, but which direct and predict resulting questions, attention, and engagement.

What You Just Learned (or, Our Attempt to Load the Above Information into Your Brain's Experience Structures, a Summary of Sorts)

- Deeply embedded *common sense*—in fact, innate property of human brain functioning—*causal reasoning* may be the most overlooked tool in the crafty screenwriter's box. The *thalamus*, deep, subcortical relay station for all sensory information, has basic survival as its goal. And survival depends on meeting our basic needs: food, shelter, etc. When our needs are met, we *feel good*, and feeling good, is connected to goals being achieved.
- Thus, screenwriters who set character goals and present challenges or threats toward achieving those goals are tapping into the very basic human pattern of *seeking cause to explain effect*.
- This reality-driven pattern underlies the success of some very good movies, but nonlinear productions—begin in the future, cut to the

now, or begin in the past and cut to the now—draw their audience into *constructing* a plausible cause-and-effect explanation.
- The *dangling cause* creates anticipation, by drawing on our insistence for causal connections. If your character states a desire, a goal, or implies a future event, your audience will hold on watching attentively for that event to take place.

Screenwriting Explorations: Cause and Effect

Knowledge of cause-and-effect sequencing is quite useful in the outlining or planning stage of writing a screenplay—that is, developing the underlying story that the screenplay will tell. In this task, the use of a "beat sheet" or "step outline" is helpful. These consist of a simple list of the scenes in the film you plan to write. It will of course be somewhat preliminary—your first attempt at seeing the whole story before you.

When you write the beat sheet, review it and check to see if all or most of the beats are causally connected (as opposed to simply being a bunch of things that happen). If there is a lack of causality across several beats, reexamining those beats is probably worthwhile. In particular, review the motive of the main character and see if he or she undertakes tasks in the service of that motive. If not, get into the shoes of the character and let him or her seek the goal.

Perceptual Prompts—Being Closer Causes Being Bigger

Size and distance are fascinating combinations of bottom-up versus top-down information flows. As seen in Chapter 1, from *Top Secret* we have existing knowledge of the size of objects in our world. We also "know" that an object farther from us will appear smaller due to distance, a concept referred to as *size constancy*.

So try this (it's harmless so ok to do at home, but you're on your own if you do this while driving)!

Hold a quarter between the fingertips of each hand, face side toward you. Position your left hand close, about twelve inches away, and your right hand fully extended arm's length away. With both eyes open, observe the two coins—they appear the same—usual quarter size; now close one eye and hold the coins at the same positions but so they appear to nearly touch. What happened to the quarter at arm's length? Did the darn thing shrink?

Your perception even knowing the quarters are not changing size based on only one eye has to tell you the farther coin is smaller! This relationship between what we know about size and what we know about distance will override truth every time.

Chapter 6

THE SCIENCE OF SHARED ATTENTION, OR, IF I WRITE A SCREENPLAY IN WHICH A TREE FALLS IN THE FOREST, AND THE READER FALLS ASLEEP HALFWAY THROUGH, HAVE I WRITTEN A SCREENPLAY?

Your screenplay or film may have stunning visuals, smart dialogue, and fascinating, multilayered characters, but if for some reason your reader or viewer tunes out, whatever brilliance displayed therein is for naught. Ultimately, the reader or viewer has to pay *attention*. As Frank Daniel said of screenwriters, "We are in the communication business, and communication isn't saying something, it's *being understood*."

Attention is the only cognitive process that carries a price; we *pay* attention. We don't pay memory or reasoning or language processes—but attention is treated as a commodity in our discourse about the brain. Psychologists have demonstrated for decades that paying attention demands mental resources. Everyone has had real-life experience in which the price demanded of attention gets too high: situations in which we get bored or overwhelmed. Under those circumstances, attention is a costly and limited mental ability.

What, exactly, *is* attention?

William James, regarded as the "Founding Father" of American Psychology, essentially established that the connection between the mental aspect of attending to a selectively few bits of our world was directly connected to our line of sight. "Millions of items ... are present to my senses which never properly enter my experience. Why? Because they have no interest for me. My experience is what I agree to attend to .... Everyone knows what attention is. It is the taking possession by the mind, in clear and vivid form, of one out of what seem several simultaneously possible objects or trains of thought ... It implies withdrawal from some things in order to deal effectively with others."[1]

1. William James, "Principles of Psychology." In *Sensation and Perception*, ed. E. B. Goldstein, p. 135 (Belmont, CA: Wadsworth, Cengage Learning, 1890/1981).

Attention is thus a form of filtering: suppressing most stimuli so as to focus on what is relevant or of interest.

The Science

When we selectively attend to a subset of available information, it is the suppression of all else going on that exhausts us. So it would seem that the best way to avoid exhausting an audience's cognition would be to provide them with a single stimulus and eliminate all distractions so the suppression of irrelevant stimuli is accomplished for them.

However, the opposite is true. A basic investigation of divided versus selective attention and some manipulations based on understanding the visual system will reveal this precious commodity to be almost completely *controllable*. Divided attention—doing more than one thing at a time—is almost always occurring in everyday life. We drive while conversing with passengers, navigating traffic, following laws, holding in mind our goal destination, and making minute corrections to acceleration and positioning of the vehicle. One might think intuitively that such apparently "distracted" driving leads to greater instances of traffic accidents; however, failures of attention occur when there has been no need for attention; long monotonous stretches of road, alone in our thoughts, is when drivers tend to get drowsy or daydream; not when taking a friend to the store or picking up children from school. Two interesting facts emerge: multitasking holds interest, thus attention; and involvement of several cognitive activities simultaneously keeps us engaged.

How, exactly, does our visual system cue into these stimuli? Our eyes move constantly. Our heads generally follow our gaze and these sources of motor responses are nearly reflexive; it takes intent to direct our eyes to focus on a specific stimulus. Remember the rods? Those receptor neurons that line the majority of the retina detecting low light (Chapter 3)? Their specialty is edges (preference is horizontal and vertical), which are created when anything, anywhere in our 180-degree visual field, moves. But it's our cones, few and tightly centered in the back of the retina, that pick up detail; when we "see" movement from our peripheral view, we turn our heads so our eyes can focus on the specifics. So three sources of moving—eyes, heads, and real-world objects that travel—are without doubt the ultimate attention getters.[2]

2. R. L. Gregory, *Eye and Brain: The Psychology of Seeing*, 5th ed. (Oxford: Oxford University Press, 1997).

Figure 6.1 Shared attention portrayed in Alfred Hitchcock's *Strangers on a Train* (1951). The onscreen characters are following the ball in a tennis match—the movement of an object that causes them to move their heads to focus those cones on that object. Meanwhile, the audience's eyes are drawn to the figure at the center, who is *not* moving, and whose presence propels the narrative. The composition and the contrast between his stillness and the movement of all the others helps filter out the irrelevant information.

In cinema, the movement of the film itself, the actors within a scene, and the objects within a scene can all create changes in viewer's eye movements—both fixations during which the viewer's eyes are held still to focus on one thing, and saccades during which the viewer's eyes are actually moving across the screen. These phenomena create a collective "shared attention" as the audience watches the moving images. Katherine J. Thomson-Jones, a professor at Oberlin College, argues that audiences are both imagining movement as well as experiencing perceptual illusions of movement.[3] Movies, a series of images presented so quickly so as to give an impression of continuous movement, prompt

---

3. K. J. Thomson-Jones, "Sensing Motion in Movies." In *Psychocinematics: Exploring Cognition at the Movies*, ed. Arthur P. Shimamura, pp. 115–32 (Oxford: Oxford University Press, 2013).

Thomson-Jones to explain that viewers are processing two metaphysical states simultaneously: the impression of movement (created by the rapid presentation of images) and the impression of images in which there is no movement. Taken together, in the screenwriting stage, the informed writer may maximize potential of holding attention by employing many types of static versus action shots.

Studies of Who's Looking Where

Psychological studies of infants being shown videos of characters attempting to achieve a goal (such as climbing up a hill) during which another character either helps by pulling the goal seeker up the hill, or hinders by pushing the goal seeker down the hill, have shown that even very young infants preferred the Helper when the goal seeker spent time gazing up the hill. This human ability to form inferences regarding another's goal state intentions may even be the basics of morality.[4] When we make eye contact with another person, we pay more attention to their words and anticipate when we are expected to make a response. Following another's gaze is a crucial adaptation we have made to predict someone's behavior and may even have been the evolutionary motivators of the unusually stark contrast between iris, sclera, and skin colors that allow us to detect gaze direction from a great distance (Tomasello et al., 2007). Figure 6.1 shows a cinematic example of shared attention—the object of attention is offscreen but we can guess it from the context, and from the sightlines of the onscreen characters.

Shared attention can be manipulated, then, by orchestrated movements of where and when a character directs their gaze. An audience watching the eye gaze of characters is deeply involved in predicting the goal state or intention of the character. By this means, shared attention becomes shared emotions, and the audience is hooked. By definition, shared emotions "facilitate coordination by the exchange of information or having emotions of the same or similar intentional structure."[5] While there is debate over a specific definition of shared emotions—no one questions that it's another human trait that ensures we empathize with or criticize those we observe based on our understanding of their emotional motivation.

4. D. U. Martin, C. Perry, and J. H. Kaufman, "An Eye on Animacy and Intention," *Frontiers in Psychology*, 7 (2016): 829.

5. J. Michael, "What Are Shared Emotions (for)?" *Frontiers in Psychology*, 7 (2016): 412.

How Filmmakers Handle Attention

Filmmakers have, since the early days of narrative cinema, instinctively worked out the problem of attention, and how to help audiences focus on important elements of the story. Figures 6.2, 6.3, and 6.4 show similar strategies employed from the 1920s to the 2010s. In these cases, a variety of visual stimuli is presented, and the camera and editing moves help the viewer filter out information that the filmmaker wants them to ignore. Although these are extreme examples, the use of composition and movement aid filmmakers in accomplishing this task more or less continuously during a film.

Screenwriters per se are relatively less concerned with issues such as composition and movement of the characters; however, they can indeed use words to suggest these visual elements. For example, screenwriter Aaron Sorkin rendered the description for Figure 6.4 as follows:

> An ultra-hip San Francisco nightclub. It's a hundred-year-old theater that's been converted into a 21st Century hot spot for Silicon Valley's rock stars. The lower level is a giant dance floor packed with sweating 20-somethings bouncing to pounding house music. There are raised blocks where scantily dressed professional dancers perform non-stop. A huge lighting grid hangs from the ceiling shooting colored lights and lasers everywhere. Also hanging from the ceiling are two trapeze bars with two performers swinging and contorting.
>
> The staircase leads up to the 2nd level which is all VIP tables that look out over the dance floor. Each VIP area has a couple of couches and a table covered in bottles of vodka, tequila, rum, mixers, ice, glasses and a private waitress who's happy to bend over and pour a drink for you.
>
> And that's where we catch up with MARK and SEAN. Sitting next to SEAN is a BEAUTIFUL WOMAN and there's another standing behind him and leaning against the couch.[6]

---

6. Aaron Sorkin, *The Social Network*. Dir. David Fincher (Columbia Pictures, 2010), p. 120.

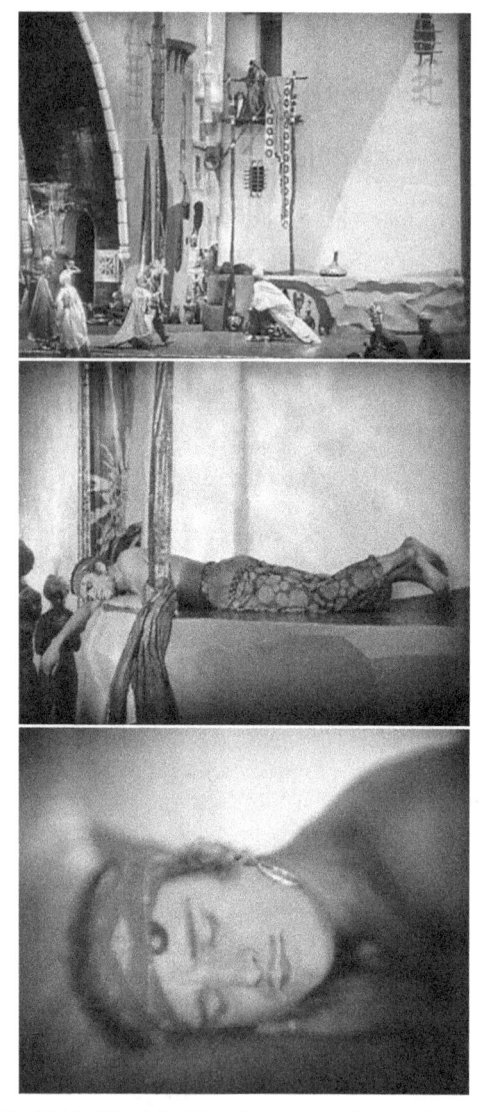

Figure 6.2 *The Thief of Baghdad* (1922) begins with a wide shot portraying a busy public square, with numerous characters, objects, and activities—a scene rich in stimuli. Soon enough, the image cuts to a closer shot of a character who was present but barely noticeable in all the stimuli—the title character, who happens also to be the main character. Soon after this, a close-up focuses on his face alone. Composition and editing thus contribute both to a stimulus-rich environment and to the filtering of superfluous stimuli.

The Science of Shared Attention 85

Figure 6.3 Lawrence is barely visible in the center right of the opening shot of this scene from *Lawrence of Arabia* (1962) but soon emerges from the clutter; the camera helps us filter out extraneous stimuli as it fastens upon him and follows his movement till he is called over to the secretary of the club. All three kinds of movement are present in this scene: camera, subject, and eye movement (the moment the viewer detects Lawrence's presence, his or her eyes move from scanning the image to focusing on him).

In a similar vein, fifty years before this, screenwriters Robert Bolt and Michael Wilson wrote this description for Figure 6.3:

LONG SHOT. The Junior Officers' Club is a spacious room, long, high, and airy, once ornate, now stripped, but immaculately clean and orderly. One side is of glass and gives onto a courtyard. Its floor is covered in bleached matting; on the walls are steel engravings of old victories, dead Generals and living Royalty. It is furnished with a great many basket chairs of uniform pattern arranged in symmetrical four round small tables with cloths of unbleached linen.

Figure 6.4 A chaotic scene that is super rich in stimuli—visual and aural—in *The Social Network* (2010). Camera movement quickly isolates the principal characters, providing the filtering.

> There is a bar and a billiard table in the foreground of the picture. Fans turn. At the bar are two or three OFFICERS. One or two OTHERS sit at tables. TWO are preparing for snooker. Otherwise the place is empty. Their voices are pleasant and well-modulated. LAWRENCE appears in the background walking through the Club alongside the glass screen.
> The SECRETARY (GIBBON) is chalking his cue at the billiard table. He is a CAPTAIN and wears a fierce moustache like a circus ring-master. The other OFFICER is also a CAPTAIN and is raising the triangular frame from the reds when the SECRETARY sees LAWRENCE, frowns, surprised, and after a fractional hesitation, calls.[7]

---

7. Robert Bolt and Michael Wilson, *Lawrence of Arabia*. Dir. David Lean (Culver City, CA: Columbia Pictures, 1962), p. 9.

In both cases, the writers draw a picture with words, then have the reader discover the salient characters in the image at the end, thus helping us filter out that which is not pertinent to the storyline.

These examples show how filmmakers have used various means to filter out extraneous stimuli in order to help the reader/viewer focus on salient elements—in each case, the main character. An extreme example of the opposite—a film with a single focus and no extraneous stimuli that must be filtered out—can be seen in Andy Warhol's *Empire* (1964) in Figure 6.5. That particular experiment has never been repeated.

From a narrative viewpoint—more concretely the realm of the screenwriter—maintaining audience attention involves a variety of tools used in combination that have already been discussed: evoking curiosity (Chapters 1 and 4), connection to a main character (Chapter 2), use of contrast (Chapter 3), and structuring a narrative around cause and effect (Chapter 5)—in addition to creating a rich enough visual experience and guiding the audience to notice the most salient or important elements of the story.

The cost of maintaining attention is most acutely felt by the audience early in the course of watching a film—during the parts most heavily loaded with exposition (the background information necessary for the audience to comprehend the story—Chapter 4). Selective attention—ignoring irrelevant information to maintain focus on one activity—is

Figure 6.5 A frame from Andy Warhol's *Empire* (1964)—eight hours of the Empire State Building between sunset and early morning. Useful for inducing sleep, but not exactly watchable.

far more demanding of cognitive resources and can only be sustained successfully for relatively brief amounts of time.

The Role of Memory

Attention is distinctly connected to memory—we have to pay attention in order to remember—and you want your reader or viewer to be able to form memories so they can update their working narrative (Chapter 1: CAM-WN model center section). Research has suggested that different types of memory require different amounts of time spent paying attention; *sensory memory* is extremely brief, thousandths of a second unless we focus, pay attention. So the color of the car you park next to at the movie theater is not likely to be remembered—the color is not important—where you park is important to remember. So you will likely make mental notes of the garage, or space number to enable successful finding of your car later. You did however see the car you parked next to, it just wasn't worth the mental effort to *encode* that car's color. *Working memory* used to be called short term, because it too is relatively brief, a half-second or so, unless the information being processed or *worked* is connected to an ongoing comprehension process. If the information in working memory is important enough or relevant to understanding what comes next, we encode that information into our long-term memory—or what we term our general knowledge—and only at this stage of memory does information begin to be *stored*.

Compare reading an article for specific details on car comparisons to reading the latest Harlan Coben novel. Motivation to learn the best car information should take precedence; buying cars is costly, a major commitment, and has long-lasting consequences—we want to pay attention to get it right. Yet, within mere minutes, we find we must reread sentences or paragraphs we just completed (see discussion in Chapter 4 of the "information dump.") Coben's mastery of the mystery novel keeps us fast forwarding, flipping pages completely immersed in absolutely nothing of real-world consequence. Why? If it were as simple as being motivated to get information right, Consumer Reports would top the bestseller lists.

Coben doesn't require we hold onto facts or numbers or even places or dates; it is the fast pace of unfolding events, character interactions, and story development that serve to mimic the relevant ease of dividing our attention—keeping us interested and engaged. The *cingulate gyre*, arched mid-line in our brains, somehow moderates our focused attention. The story enters through sensory memory—as words flying past the reader's eyes—information enters working memory and is rapidly stored by connecting to the reader's general knowledge—and becomes part of the reader's working narrative—available for cross-checking and reference at any point as the story unfolds. For the screenwriter, this opens the toy box of grabbing and directing the viewer's visual focus.

The Challenge of Short Films

One form of filmmaking impacted by the high cost of audience attention is the short film. The short—five to thirty-five or so minutes—is the standard focus of film production at film schools the world over. It is, however, an archaic form. Initially, all films were shorts. From the 1890s to the 1910s, the stand-alone short film—a few minutes to eight or ten minutes in length—dominated cinema. In the 1910s, though, Hollywood film production diverged in two directions—the full-length feature film and the serial—what we now call a *series*. These two forms remain standard a hundred years later.

One would think that with distribution channels now available on the Internet, short films would make a comeback, but this is not the case: feature films and series dominate the Internet, too. Given so many possibilities available for viewing, why have the Hollywood models of the 1910s persisted, while the short film has not?

One clue lies in the relative cost of attention demanded by the exposition in the early part of a film, compared to the emotional payoff the film delivers. In a feature film of 120 minutes, the first thirty or so—corresponding to the "First Act" or *setup*—are the most cognitively demanding, since the audience must pay attention in order to absorb the who, what, when, where, and why of the story. Once the energy has been expended, though, the rest of the film—three-quarters of it—is free to deliver its emotional payload with relatively fewer cognitive demands. For example, once we invest our energy into learning who the characters are in *The Hangover* (2009), their relationships, what's going on in their lives, why they are in Las Vegas, and find them in the predicament of waking up after a night of partying confronted by a series of mysteries—not the least of which is the whereabouts of the bridegroom—we can proceed to enjoy the emotional payoff that results for the rest of the film with relatively few cognitive demands placed on us.

In contrast, anyone who has attended a film festival to view an evening of short films recognizes how exhausting the experience can be. The viewer of the short film must withstand the cognitive demands of exposition repeatedly throughout the evening, with proportionately little emotional payoff. By its very nature—being short—the short film can never compete with the feature because of these meager returns on investment of emotional energy.

For television series, the ratio of time spent expending energy on exposition to time spent reaping the emotional rewards is even more lopsided. Once we have gotten to know Jerry, Elaine, George, Kramer, and their basic circumstances in *Seinfeld*, the series can run for almost a decade with few cognitive demands placed on us.

The Challenge of Virtual Reality

Filmmakers have traditionally had significant control over aiding the viewer in filtering extraneous stimuli, because they have control over what the camera captures. This is not the case in the emerging Virtual Reality form. The immersive experience has great potential in the area of gaming, since it allows greater control of the action by the viewer—interaction with the medium. However, traditional narrative is a challenge because the creator has significantly less control over what the viewer actually sees. The viewer can turn his or her head in addition to moving his or her eyes. Critical narrative information—a character hiding a knife, for instance, or surreptitiously leaving a door unlocked—may be missed by a viewer who happens to be looking the other way at the moment the information is revealed.

Filmmakers interested in doing narrative in this form will likely have to adapt, perhaps using the techniques of the stage, another dramatic form in which the storytellers have relatively less control over the focus of audience attention than in cinema. Another technique present in both cinema and theater is the repetition of key narrative information such as in *recapitulation* scenes.

What You Just Learned (or, Our Attempt to Load the Above Information into Your Brain's Experience Structures, a Summary of Sorts)

- A cognitive resource that carries a price tag, *attention* can be *selective* or *divided*, and the savvy screenwriter understands the audience can only pay so much at a time. Just as distracted driving

may result in accidents, worse is the long stretch of straight road—your audience needs to be able to *focus* on what is key to your narrative story line and *filter* what is not pertinent.
- *Eye movements* are mostly involuntary. Our rods fire to the slightest suggestion of movement, causing us to then move our heads, in order to *focus* our cones, which fire to fine, detailed information, so we can identify the source of movement. This creates three sources of movement—eyes—heads—and the real-world object that is zipping past us—like the tiny space ships from *Star Wars*. Thus, *movement* is the ultimate attention getter. Write your script to alternate or mingle static and action shots.
- *Other's eye movements* also directs our attention. If your actor is gazing at something or someone or even off stage—your audience will also attend to that object or direction. Evolution has colored our iris to be in contrast with the white of our eye and we attend to what others are looking at—*shared attention* in a movie is easily manipulated by characters gaze.

Screenwriting Explorations: Resetting Attention

In the course of reading a script you have written, note where it seems to bog down, or where your attention seems to wander. If you give it to others to read, note where they report this experience. Because paying attention is a demanding activity, check to see how long the scenes are. Scenes tend to last about three minutes—and in script form three pages—before the movie or script switches away to another location, or a change in circumstances occurs—a new character entering, for instance. These changes allow for the brain to refresh and reset, and then pay attention once more. If your scenes are too long or their content too stagnant, consider breaking them up or cutting them down.

Perceptual Prompts—Shared Attention Depends on How Well You Know the Speaker

People say the very same word in countless variations—yet, usually anyone can understand what is being said. Wide variation in acoustic signals are overcome by our drive to comprehend; so slurred speech or sloppy pronunciations are "understood" despite incomplete information.

Do this with a close friend and then with a clerk at the grocery store:

Say "This was a best buy." "Did you go to the store" "What are you doing?"
Notice your tongue as you speak to your friend. Did you say 'best buy' or 'bes buy'? Was the pause between 'did you' longer to create clarity for the unfamiliar clerk? 'Did you' often becomes "dijoo" between friends. Analysis of speech has demonstrated we all take more care in articulating when we are strangers—a savvy screenwriter will consider character relationships and levels of intimacy in writing dialogue. (Kellogg, 2013)

Chapter 7

THE SCIENCE OF CONFLICT, OR, WHAT'S WRONG WITH WATCHING TWO HOURS OF PEOPLE JUST GETTING ALONG AND HELPING EACH OTHER?

It seems that when it comes to writing drama, everyone is talking about *conflict*. "The perfect hero is the one who offers the most conflict in the situation" (Blake Snyder);[1] "The essential nature of the drama is conflict and suspense" (Gustav Freytag);[2] "Conflict is one element that seems to be an essential ingredient of every forceful dramatic work" (David Howard);[3] "A Story Event creates meaningful change in the life situation of a character that is expressed and experienced in terms of a value and ACHIEVED THROUGH CONFLICT" (Robert McKee);[4] "All drama is conflict" (Syd Field).[5] Even the French are in on it: *"Le drame, en général, c'est une représentation de la volonté de l'homme en conflit avec les puissances mystérieuses our les forces naturelles qui nous limitent et nous rapetissent"* (Drama is a representation of the will of man in conflict with the mysterious powers or natural forces which limit and belittle us [Ferdinand Brunetiere]).[6]

1. Blake Snyder, *Save the Cat* (Studio City, CA: Michael Wiese Productions, 2005), p. 64.
2. Gustav Freytag, *The Technique of the Drama: An Exposition of Dramatic Composition and Art*, trans. E. J. MacEwan, p. 109 (Chicago, IL: Scott Foresman, 1900).
3. David Howard and Edward Mabley, *The Tools of Screenwriting* (New York: St. Martin's Griffin, 1995), p. 46.
4. Robert McKee, *Story: Style, Structure, Substance, and the Principles of Screenwriting* (New York: HarperCollins, 1997), pp. 34–5.
5. Syd Field, *Screenplay: The Foundations of Screenwriting* (New York: Random House, 2005), p. 25.
6. Ferdinand Brunetiere, *Etudes Critiques*, vol. VII (Paris: Librairie Hachette et Cie, 1903), p. 152.

Figure 7.1 Conflict at the micro (scene) level: Pat wants some information but Principal Nancy Metger is terrified of him. From *Silver Linings Playbook* (2011). Conflict can be seen at three different levels in many successful films: scene, sequence, and the film overall.

What these writers mean by conflict is that a character who wants something must overcome an obstacle to get it. And it exists not only on the level of the script as a whole, but also in subunits of sequence[7] and scene[8] ("What is the conflict in the scene?" is one of the question David Howard suggests a writer ask when writing a scene, right after "whose scene is it?").[9]

For example, in *Silver Linings Playbook* (2011), the main conflict involves Pat's desire to reconnect with this ex-wife Nikki. The obstacles to this outcome, which create conflict, involve Pat's restraining order, and the fact that she's moved away, and moved on in her life, and he has no way to reach her. In the second sequence, though, his objective is to *prepare* to win her back, as opposed to *win* her back. This involves getting into shape and reading from her English class reading list. Conflict arises from the skepticism of those around him, and in one case, his disagreement with the ending of one of the books. On the

---

7. Sequences are defined as "eight- to fifteen-minute segments of film that have their own internal structure—in effect, shorter films built inside the larger film. To a significant extent, each sequence has its own protagonist, tension, rising action and resolution." See P. J. Gulino (2004), *Screenwriting: The Sequence Approach* (New York: Bloomsbury, 2004).

8. In general, a scene is defined as action that takes place in one location continuously, identified in the "master scene" screenplay format by a scene heading.

9. Howard and Mabley, *The Tools of Screenwriting*, p. 93.

smallest level—the dramatic scene—Pat confronts his former principal Nancy Metgers in the middle of the sequence. He wants to talk to her to let her know he's available to return to work, and to find out if Nikki still teaches at the school. The conflict arises from Nancy's fear of him and thus her attempt to cut the conversation short and flee to safety (see Figure 7.1). Conflict at three levels: film, sequence, scene.[10]

It's relatively easy to see why conflict would do such wonders for dramatists—if a character wants something and there is doubt about that character getting it, and—this is critical—the audience has established sympathy or even identity with a character in the scene so he or she actually *cares* about the outcome (see Chapter 2)—that audience can be held in suspense, between hope that the character will achieve the goal and fear that he or she won't (see the discussion of endorphin release upon achieving goals in Chapter 5).

Obviously, if there were no conflict—no obstacle to the character achieving his or her objective—it's hard to generate suspense. Imagine if Moses had asked Pharaoh to let his people go, and Pharaoh responded to the affirmative and offered extra supplies and departing gifts? What if Buzz had never shown up in Andy's room and Woody remained top toy, with no rivals, throughout *Toy Story*? What if Colonel Quaritch decided the Na'vi creatures ought to be left alone in peace in *Avatar* and the humans left the planet, leaving only parting gifts? A significant reason for tuning in would be absent.

Another reason that conflict may evoke audience attention is its relative rarity in life. The normal processes of life: taking a walk, eating a meal, etc., seldom involve significant conflicts. They become the experiences that human attention normally filters out. Our attention tends to be drawn more to stimuli that are a *contrast* to normal, routine stimuli, and the portrayal of conflict is a natural attention-getter (see Chapter 3 on contrast). In this vein, director Alfred Hitchcock said, "Some films

---

10. This iterative structure can be seen as a *fractal*—a structure in which similar patterns recur at progressively smaller scales—a phenomenon seen throughout the natural world (the structure of a fern is a good example). This structure is analyzed to the level of individual shots in James E. Cutting, Jordan E. DeLong, and Christine E. Nothelfer, "Attention and the Evolution of Hollywood Film," *Psychological Science* (2009), doi:10.1177/0956797610361679. Also discussed by David Pincus (2010), "And the Oscar Goes to … Our Brains?" *Psychology Today* (2010), retrieved from https://www.psychologytoday.com/blog/the-chaotic-life/201003/and-the-oscar-goes-toour-brains).

are slices of life, mine are slices of cake." Presumably the "slice of life" film is life presented as it is—generally dull.

The Science of Conflict

One clue to the use of conflict to engage an audience can be found in evolution. Evolutionary biologist Edward O. Wilson opined that "the great gift of the conscious human brain is the capacity—and with it the irresistible inborn drive—to build scenarios."[11] This is a useful adaptation because it allows us to imagine various possible outcomes of a course of action very quickly before we make a decision about what action to take. Should one ask a coworker out on a date? Before taking such an action, it's an advantage to weigh various scenarios that may result. She might say yes, and the date might go successfully, resulting in a blossoming relationship. However, what if the relationship sours? Will I be able to function as her coworker? What if it sours and she is later promoted to be my boss? What if I sour on her and end it and then she becomes my boss? What if she says no, and I have to deal with her as a coworker? Or a boss? What if *I* become the boss? Will I be accused of sexual harassment? What if it turns out she's going out with *my* boss? The reality of our daily lives is that a single action yields a great many hypothetical outcomes, and it's to our advantage to generate those hypothetical scenarios rapidly and constantly so we can weigh the likely outcomes of that action and thus make the wisest choice.

Filmmakers and screenwriters can utilize conflict in their stories because the uncertainty of an outcome of a conflict situation triggers this propensity in the viewer or reader to construct hypothetical scenarios. In such a case, the viewer is not participating as a decision maker, but as a witness to the choices that onscreen characters face and the decisions they make.

Conflict Deep within Us

Conflict exists on a number of levels in human perceptual-cognitive systems.

---

11. Edward O. Wilson, *The Social Conquest of Earth* (New York: W. W. Norton, 2012), p. 82.

Figure 7.2 Philosopher and cognitive scientist Jerry Fodor espoused the notion that our sense organs are individual modules whose information can become entangled in our subcortical brain structures, resulting in conflicting interpretations and impulses.

One place to begin is in the morning: conflict begins immediately for most of us when our mind becomes aware of the morning alarm clock and our body refuses to get out of bed. This conflict provides a simple example of the constant battle between our central nervous system—focused on higher cognitive processes—and our peripheral nervous system—focused on funneling the external real world as it is right now—to our brains.

One view of the mind–body conflict comes from early perceptual psychologist Jerry Fodor in a 1983 article, which suggested that our sensory systems are individual modules; the fact that light can only be transduced by rods and cones—no amount of light shone into one's ear will be seen, and so for sound—the changes in air pressure against our skin will never be heard. This specific input to output, which Fodor[12] calls *modularity*, is direct; that is, our eyes and ears change the real-world energy into nerve impulses without interpretation or judgment. But all incoming real-world information passes first through our subcortical emotion brain centers (from which emerges our sense of "mind"), which may be our "mind," after which point nothing is direct. The raw stimuli of light and sound become more useful to us. For example, raw information from our eyes about steam rising from fresh baked bread means nothing in particular till such data is combined with stored memory and we instantly understand that the fresh baked bread is going to taste delicious. Look again at the CAM-WN model (Chapter 1)—all those input items at the bottom are available to the informed screenwriter—and once bottom-up is in, your audience will helplessly begin to speculate and wonder how the current conflict is going to end.

However, raw information can be processed in very complicated ways. Someone's thought processes may be the following, upon seeing a figure approaching: *I see a person. That person is my mother* (subcortical brain compares stimulus with stored memory of mother). *Oh no! What should I buy for her birthday gift?* (recognition of mother triggers another association in the subcortical brain) *Did she see my hesitation? She's not smiling! Say something before she cries!* (concern over birthday gift triggers further associations based on memory of past conflicts). A simple visual stimulus thus leads to a complicated and potentially conflicted reaction.

Audiences respond not just to the sound and sights of the cinema, but also with all the accumulated experience of their own lives and their exposure to movies (see Chapter 1 on constructivist psychology). Bottom-up processing (light enters the eye, is transduced, travels to visual cortex) is thus perfunctorily hijacked by top-down recognition and guilt, fear, and other reactions ensue.

A useful example of conflict in information flows can be seen in Figure 7.3.

Two sets of arrows exhibit the Müller-Lyer optical illusion, created by German sociologist Franz Carl Müller-Lyer (1857–1916). The set on the bottom shows that all the shafts of the arrows are of the same length.

---

12. N. Smith, "Dissociation and Modularity: Reflections on Language and Mind." In *Mind, Brain and Language*, ed. M. Banich and M. Mack (Mahwah, NJ: Lawrence Erlbaum, 2003).

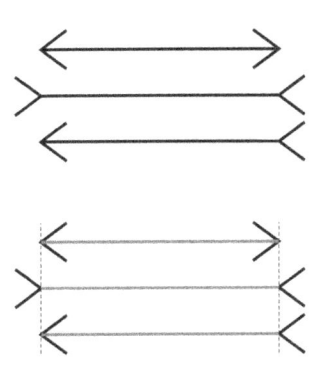

Figure 7.3 The Müller-Lyer Illusion, providing conflict for our cognitive-perceptual systems since 1889.

First glance at the three lines in the Müller-Lyer Illusion elicit the assumption that one is longer than the others. Then after measuring and assuring ourselves they are identical in length, we can attempt to "see" them as equal. We fail. This illusion is a direct result of top-down conflict with bottom-up information—in this case, no amount of knowledge can override the evolutionary bias that insists that open-ended angles extend distance. We know the truth but can't see it. So from the get-go, conflict is a brain by-product of dealing with reality.

The Emotional Roller-Coaster

The human brain operates under a regime of frequent inner conflict, and that conflict can be provoked by filmmakers through various techniques, especially those found in Chapter 3 on contrast.

Fear versus trust, despair versus hope—each carries a different neurochemical signature. For example, remember the familiar adrenaline rush evoked in Chapter 1 when a strange dog's growls had you up a tree? That rush is ameliorated by our amygdala, deep in our brains, releasing a *counter chemical* that restores normal breathing and provides us a feeling that we are safe. This battle between brain chemicals, like the conflict between hoping for a goal outcome to be achieved and fearing failure or loss, rages relentlessly until some resolution, some state of relief is achieved.

That can be a powerful screenwriting tool—evoke conflict between characters or within one—and your audience's neural chemistry will respond; thus, your viewers become emotionally engaged on a molecular level causing adrenaline, dopamine, and other excitatory chemicals to begin flooding the synapses. And while there is no predicting exactly what resulting emotion the viewer will identify with most, those neurotransmitters in abundance guarantee an acute attentive state. Skillful modulation of tension and release (see Chapter 3) may ease one conflict or bring temporary relief, slowing heart rate and breathing, and allow the viewer to sense success. This momentary break in heart pounding also allows intellectual recovery—so the narrative may support speculation or reflection appropriately. Timing is critical; the brain is a quick instrument to play: one sigh of successful relief bids the next moment of trauma alert.

In this tension-and-release pattern, attention is sustained without sacrificing comprehension, and not only will your audience be raptly engaged, but also they'll eagerly tell others your movie is a must-see.

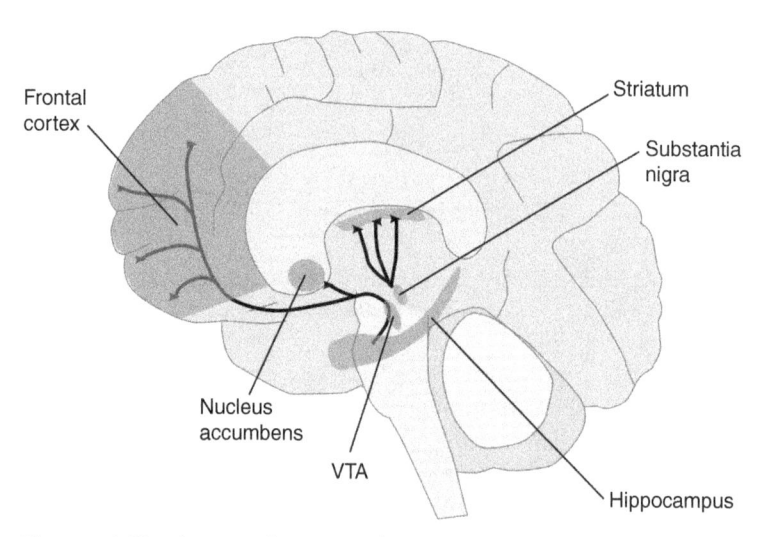

Figure 7.4 Your brain on dopamine. The emotions one feels, provoked by various stimuli, are expressions of chemicals. As the stimuli change and contrast, *counter chemicals* counteract the effect of whatever chemical is dominant at the moment. Your brain is thus riven by conflict on a microscopic as well as a macro level. (NIDA/ Quasihuman).

Verbal Conflict

Humans have evolved as social creatures, and our capacity to "read" the intentions—and indeed character—of others, is central to both survival and the smooth operation of society. Conversational conflict in dialogue exploits the audience's predisposition to do this, leading viewers to mentally build their understanding of characters on many levels—not the least of which is the character's intent or desire. Representing goals that are opposing (or shared against a mutual foe) also adds detail for the viewer regarding that character's morals and life history, because these can readily be reflected in the tactics used in that conflict. These conversational tidbits weave into building the working narrative that the viewer is actively constructing. Further, by making such insights less explicitly stated, viewers are activated to infer their understanding of the character's intentions, goal states, and views of the world through clues.

In *The Social Conquest of Earth*, evolutionary biologist Edward O. Wilson argues that the advantage humans gained by living in groups around a campfire required the development of social skills unknown before by any other species, including the division of labor, the sharing of food, and the securing of a mate.

> All of these pressures confer an advantage on those able to read the intention of others, grow in the ability to gain trust and alliance, and manage rivals. Social intelligence was therefore always at a high premium. A sharp sense of empathy can make a huge difference, and with it an ability to manipulate, to gain cooperation, and to deceive.[13]

We are thus primed to seek clues that can yield these insights into others. A famous example of conflict dialogue that yields insight into intent and character can be seen in *Double Indemnity* (1944), in which Walter Neff arrived at the house of one of his customers Mr. Dietrichson in order to get a renewal on an auto insurance policy, instead encounters Dietrichson's wife Phyllis, in whom he takes a liking.

> **PHYLLIS:** Mr. Neff, why don't you drop by tomorrow evening about eight-thirty. He should be in by then.
> **NEFF:** Who?
> **PHYLLIS:** My husband. You were anxious to talk to him weren't you?

13. Wilson, *The Social Conquest of Earth*, pp. 43–4.

NEFF: Sure, only I'm getting over it a little, if you know what I mean.
PHYLLIS: There's a speed limit in this state, Mr. Neff. Forty-five miles an hour.
NEFF: How fast was I going, officer?
PHYLLIS: I'd say about ninety.
NEFF: Suppose you get down off your motor-cycle and give me a ticket.
PHYLLIS: Suppose I let you off with a warning this time.
NEFF: Suppose it doesn't take.
PHYLLIS: Suppose I have to whack you over the knuckles.
NEFF: Suppose I bust out crying and put my head on your shoulder.
PHYLLIS: Suppose you try putting it on my husband's shoulder.
NEFF: That tears it.[14]

Here, the objectives of the characters are clear and in conflict: he wants her, and she wants to deny him. Neff's obstacles are not only her intransigence but also the fact that society prohibits such an encounter, as she is married. This forces him to use an indirect tactic—speaking metaphorically. This allows him both to make a pass at her and to be able to deny he did. Such an approach yields information not only about Neff's intent, but also his character—willing to break society's rules—and his cleverness in being able to pursue his objective without exposing himself to subsequent social attack. Without the conflicts presented in the scene, such information would be impossible for the audience to glean.

Conflict woven into vocabulary choices or vocal quality enhances full-bodied mental representations. But conflict can also be created by nature; "mere human confronts a mile-wide tornado" sort of thing. This form of conflict relies on viewers' real-world knowledge that people are no match for the forces of nature, and the writer can use more action, more visual information, to create the same depth of character understanding in viewers.

On a very basic level, the human brain is designed, in large part, to detect speech sounds and to comprehend language. We are the only creatures whose auditory cortex begins before birth to develop a sorting area (called the *parabelt*) in which sounds within a particular amplitude

---

14. Billy Wilder and Raymond Chandler, *Double Indemnity*, dir. Billy Wilder (Paramount Pictures, 1944), pp. 11–12.

Figure 7.5 Phyllis and Walter discuss traffic law enforcement—or is it sexual impropriety? A scene containing conflicted (or *indirect*) dialogue in *Double Indemnity* (1944).

and frequency are separated for further consideration, and if these sounds follow the "rules" of speech, humans have developed a critical language area of the auditory cortex that attaches meaning to these sounds. Voices strained above other sounds in a scene (like music backgrounds, crowd noise, or crash/burn/exploding sounds) are successfully received by most audience members, as our brains prefer meaning and for us that means detecting spoken language above the din. In detecting emotion and meaning, schemas—top-down processing—also play a role. A shout in the middle of a quiet conversation, above the normal speech decibel range, can be identical in its physical properties (decibels and hertz) to a shout at a loud party. In one context, panic may be the inferred emotion, in the other, simply the need to be heard.

Conflicted Human Nature

Characters who have inner conflicts have been at the center of stories since Achilles brooded alone by the ships while his comrades got the worst of it in Homer's *Iliad*. Certainly Pat in *Silver Linings Playbook* battles through inner conflict, as does R. P. McMurphy and several other characters in *One Flew Over the Cuckoo's Nest*.

Lawrence of *Lawrence of Arabia* is riven by inner conflict—loyalties to his army versus loyalty to the Arabs, revulsion for and love of violence, his almost supernatural vision of himself versus his mortal limits. Late in the first half of the film, his inner conflicts erupt as he confesses to executing an Arab allied with the British cause:

> Now we see LAWRENCE utterly in the grip of his contradictions. His face works and he twists slowly about in his chair as he gropes for words.[15]

Edward O. Wilson looks to the unique way that humans evolved to discover a fundamental and—he believes, unchangeable—contradiction that manifests itself in human nature universally: *multilevel evolution*. Most species of animals evolve at one level, either as individuals looking out for themselves or, much more rarely, as part of a group with which they cooperate instinctively (such as ants).

However, humans evolved both to look out for themselves in society (individual selection) and to look out for society as a whole (group selection). Both levels of selection must be functional for the human species to survive. The problem is that they are opposites. Individual selection favors individuals whose behavior is competitive and selfish, whereas group selection favors groups whose members exhibit generosity and altruism. These two impulses are thus in constant conflict.

A classic illustration of this occurs any time a group of friends dines at a restaurant and decides to split the check equally. It's in everyone's individual interest to order the most expensive thing on the menu, since others will chip in and subsidize the expense, and the individual who thus orders treats himself or herself to the best meal at the best price. However, it's in the *group's* interest for individuals to order something more modest, since that will reduce the cost for the group as a whole. The answer to this quandary is that there is no answer; different individuals will approach the problem in different, conflicting ways, possibly causing more than one friendship to dissolve in the process.

With respect to the creative arts, Wilson concludes:

> An inevitable result of the mutually offsetting forces of multilevel selection is permanent ambiguity in the individual human mind, leading

---

15. Robert Bolt and Michael Wilson, *Lawrence of Arabia*, dir. David Lean (Culver City, CA: Columbia Pictures, 1962), p. 127.

to countless scenarios among people in the way they bond, love, affiliate, betray, share, sacrifice, steal, deceive, redeem, punish, appeal, and adjudicate. The struggle endemic to each person's brain, mirrored in the vast superstructure of cultural evolution, is the fountainhead of the humanities. A Shakespeare in the world of ants, untroubled by any such war between honor and treachery, and chained by the rigid commands of instinct to a tiny repertory of feeling, would be able to write only one drama of triumph and one of tragedy. Ordinary people, on the other hand, can invent an endless variety of such stories, and compose an infinite symphony of ambience and mood.[16]

Dialogue: On the Nose and off the Rails

Often screenwriters are instructed to avoid *on the nose* dialogue at all costs. Robert McKee describes it thus: "writing dialogue and activity in which a character's deepest thoughts and feelings are expressed by what the character says and does."[17] Blake Snyder describes it as "obvious, unfunny, and something we've seen before."[18]

To provide an example, McKee's poses a hypothetical scene:

> Two attractive people sit opposite each other at a candlelit table, the light glinting off the crystal wine-glasses and the dewy eyes of the lovers. Soft breezes billow the curtains. A Chopin nocturne plays in the background. The lovers reach across the table, touch hands, look longingly in each other's eyes, say, "I love you, I love you" … and actually mean it. This is an unactable scene and will die like a rat in the road.[19]

McKee's advice for avoiding such dialogue is to recognize that dialogue must have *subtext*.

An actor brings a character to life from the inside out, from unspoken, even unconscious thoughts and feelings out to a surface of behavior. The actors will say and do whatever the scene requires, but

---

16. Wilson, *The Social Conquest of Earth*, p. 274.
17. McKee, *Story*, p. 253.
18. Snyder, *Save the Cat*, p. 189.
19. McKee, *Story*, p. 253.

they find their sources for creation in the inner life. The scene above is unactable because it has no inner life, no subtext.[20]

Although McKee does not make clear *why* two individuals who love each other could never realistically express their inner thoughts when they say so, he nonetheless suggests the scene would be actable if the couple is changing a tire and discussing *that*, leaving the actors to find the love.

A more useful way of thinking about avoiding "on the nose" dialogue is to see it not as an issue of subtext but rather "indirect speech" or *indirection*. Tools for creating indirect speech are readily available through the use of time-tested rhetorical devices such as metaphor, simile, hyperbole, metonymy, and irony. These devices set up a conflict between the words used and the meanings conveyed, and come naturally to human beings due to a variety of situations in which they convey information and negotiate relationships.

> Human language is shot through with irony, a fine-tuned play of hyperbole and misdirection that conveys a meaning different from that in the phrase as literally worded. Language can be indirect, insinuating a message instead of stating it baldly, and thereby leaving open plausible deniability. Examples include overt, even clichéd sexual come-ons ("Would you like to come up and see my etchings?"); polite requests ("If you could help me change this flat tire, I'd be eternally grateful"); threats ("Nice store you got here. Be a shame if something happened to it"); bribes ("Gee, officer, would it be possible for me to pay the ticket right here?"); soliciting a donation ("We hope you will join our Leadership Program").[21]

Examples of such indirection in dialogue abound in cinema. The scene from *Double Indemnity*, quoted earlier, involves the use of metaphor. Ernst Lubitsch, the great director of comedy in the 1930s and 1940s, was known for his "Lubitsch Touch," which was really simply a facility with such indirection, often involving the socially explosive subject of sex. For example, in *Trouble in Paradise* (1932), on which Lubitsch collaborated with screenwriter Samson Raphaelson, a

---

20. McKee, *Story*, p. 253.
21. Wilson, *The Social Conquest of Earth*, p. 230.

society woman and François, at a party, discuss Monsieur Laval, who has recently become the personal secretary of Mariette, the rich heiress to a cosmetic company.

LADY: That's that M'sieu Laval.
FRANÇOIS: Laval? Who is M'sieu Laval?
LADY: *I* don't know. *She* says he's her secretary.
François turns and looks searchingly at Gaston, who has paused with Mariette at another group.
FRANÇOIS: Oh? So.
LADY: And *he* says he's her secretary. Maybe I'm wrong. Maybe he *is* her secretary. (She laughs cynically).[22]

The "on the nose" version of dialogue here might simply have the Lady say, "That's M'seiu Laval, and even though he claims to be Mariette's secretary, I think they are having sex." However, such an approach could potentially damage her relationships with others in her social circle. Instead, by use of indirection—outwardly saying one thing but communicating a message in conflict with it—she has *plausible deniability*. Taken out of context, her words are innocent.

Irony is perhaps the most powerful—and easiest to use—of rhetorical devices and is unique in that it involves a character saying two completely opposite things at the same time. A good example can be found in *Toy Story*, when Woody confronts Buzz, who is getting into the routines of Andy's room.

WOODY: You actually think you're THE "Buzz Lightyear?" Oh, all this time I thought it was an act. (to the room) Hey, guys! Look! It's the REAL Buzz Lightyear!
BUZZ: You're mocking me, aren't you?
WOODY: Oh, no, no, no.[23]

By "no, no, no," of course, Woody actually means "yes." Meanwhile, in his other lines, it is clear he means the opposite of what he says: he

---

22. Samson Raphaelson, *Three Screen Comedies* (Madison: University of Wisconsin Press, 1983), pp. 118–19.
23. John Lasseter et al., *Toy Story*, dir. John Lasseter (Pixar Animation Studios and Walt Disney Pictures, 1995), p. 36.

Figure 7.6 Woody uses irony to attack Buzz in *Toy Story* (1995). Irony is the easiest of the rhetorical devices a writer can use to avoid "on the nose" dialogue, and it is an exquisite expression of conflict: a character speaking ironically is saying two opposite things at the same time.

does *not* think it's all a joke, and then does *not* believe Buzz is the "real" Buzz Lightyear.

It's worth noting that one of Buzz's characteristics is that he's incapable of irony. Because most people are readily capable of detecting and using irony in everyday life, Buzz's incapacity reflects his rigidity and renders him easy to make fun of.

Aaron Sorkin makes masterful use of indirect dialogue in *The Social Network* (2010). When Mark tells the attorney of Divya, Tyler, and Cameron, "I think if your clients want to sit on my shoulders and call themselves tall they have a right to give it a try," he is speaking metaphorically, as is Erica when she tells Mark, "The internet's not written in pencil, Mark, it's written in ink." When Sean tells Mark "This is a once-in-a-generation-holy-shit idea and the water under the Golden Gate is freezing cold," he is employing *metonymy*—using the attribute of something to represent the thing meant—in this case, the place where the founder of Victoria's Secret committed suicide because he sold out too soon and lost hundreds of millions of dollars. When Tyler tells Cameron and Divya, after discovering that Mark has expanded Facebook to include more colleges, "that Cease and Desist letter really scared the shit out of him, huh?" he is being ironic—what he means is, of course, that the Cease and Desist letter was not effective at all.[24]

The use of such indirection is a good way to avoid "on the nose" dialogue, and unleashes conflict that dovetails well with our highly conflicted perceptual and cognitive processes.

What You Just Learned (or, Our Attempt to Load the Above Information into Your Brain's Experience Structures, a Summary of Sorts)

- Of all ingredients for a successful screenplay, *conflict is essential*—the protagonist must overcome some obstacle. This is key not just for the whole story, but also conflict must be woven into every sequence, every scene. Ask yourself, *Who's scene is it?*
- Conflict is the *brain-body* relationship—it's the very fact that our body is receiving sensory information and sending it up to our brains, while our brains are interpreting, adding top-down—opposite flows up information—means humans, your readers or viewers, are built to thrive on challenges.
- How does this information help a screenwriter? The viewer is ready, well practiced in battle, so writing conflict into every scene is highly simpatico with our perceptual/cognitive system.
- If your audience is emotionally connected to your protagonist, and your main man (or woman) is facing obstruction to their goals, your audience is experiencing *emotional conflict*—hope that your character achieves his or her goal—and fear that failure is possible.
- Movies are not real—that's why we love them—real is ho-hum, day-in-day-out, not a lot of conflict; so there is audience expectation of clear and present danger—don't let them down.
- Human reasoning has a propensity to think forward; that is, we hypothesize all kinds of possible outcomes for any given situation. When we are involved in your story, your characters' dilemma becomes our mental exploration of all possible outcomes—we are invested. An invested audience is a box office dream.

---

24. Aaron Sorkin, *The Social Network*, dir. David Fincher (Columbia Pictures, 2010), pp. 74, 78, 122, 82.

- Every emotion has a *neurochemical signature*, which accompanies our feelings and influences how we relate to our world. Adrenaline arouses flight or fight, while serotonin bids acceptance of all things right—*timing of conflict and release* turns these biological signals on–off, so consider your scenes, and make timing align with audience neurochemistry.
- Verbal conflict—arguments work, but hints, or *indirect speech*, evoke reader or viewer to infer—and when humans are drawing *inferences* to support comprehension they are involved in what's coming next. Avoid on-the-nose dialogue by use of such tools such as *irony* and *metonymy* and your audience's *specialized auditory cortex* will seek meaning.

Screenwriting Explorations: Conflict on the Scene Level

In writing your scenes, even in a first draft, it's extremely useful to identify the "main character" of the scene, what he or she wants, and the obstacle to that objective. This generates the conflict that in turn generates anticipation in readers, and keeps them turning the pages. After the first draft, study a given scene to see if you can find its "culmination" and "resolution." These are usually opposites. In a seduction scene, the culmination may be the moment we think the seduction will succeed, and the resolution (at the end) is when we learn it won't. Such a structure in dramatic scenes not only exploits the conflict inherent in the situation, but it also uses contrast to maintain audience focus.

Perceptual Prompts—Brain on Conflict, or the Missing Phoneme Effect

Warren (1970) had participants listen to sentences that were interrupted by a cough or other nonspeech sound. None of the listeners could report even hearing the cough—everyone filled in the missing speech sound. He did his experiment again with psychology faculty, who know very well the influence of top-down processes to fill in missing information in order to make sense of what they are hearing—and again, not one person reported hearing the cough. Our brains just omit what doesn't make sense (Goldstein, 2007).

Chapter 8

THE SCIENCE OF IMAGINATION: TEMPORAL LOBES, HOW TO THINK CREATIVELY, STAGES OF MIND, OR, YOUR DOPE-FUELED IMAGININGS

Scientists, everyone knows, are analytical, precise, and use their left brain; creative types are free-spirited, disorganized, and use their right brain. Scientists observe the physical world; screenwriters explore the ephemeral world of their imaginations. Anyway, that may be a popular mythology.

In fact, screenwriting, like science, is born of observation. Those who observe life—the behavior of humans, the process of living, indeed by all creatures—engage their mental powers in explaining that which they observe. Noted Broadway director Jose Quintero once noted, "Drama is the study of the inner life of human beings."[1]

As often as not, humans and other creatures do not appear to be rational in pursuit of their goal state, which is the end stage of a sequence of actions necessary and sufficient to achieve a goal. It is up to the writer and the scientist to develop causal explanations for that which they observe. After all, human brains are predisposed to seek understanding of what the cause is and what the effect is (see Chapter 5). This underlying beginning of both storytelling and hypothesis testing; our observations of our world; and our emotions, thoughts, and behaviors to obtain goals gives rise to objectives common to both science and drama: to express to the world how we see things making sense. As scientists, a very well-tested method of hypothesis development and rigorous counter-testing, provides a platform to assert causal explanations for our observations. For screenwriters, the method of storytelling, much older than science, is testing and counter-testing in a most demanding form: the response of an audience, which viscerally determines the extent to which the creator has spoken the truth about the human condition—their own condition.

1. Jose Quintero, *Lecture* (New York: Columbia University, October 1980).

The notion that the right brain hemisphere governs creativity while the left brain hemisphere supports language and analytical reasoning has been resoundingly overturned in our era of neuroimaging evidence. Many researchers (Storm and Patel, 2014; Kounios and Beeman, 2009) provide imaging evidence that both hemispheres are differentially active during problem solving and, in fact, when participants are expressly instructed to be "creative," the release of dopamine in the bilateral temporal lobes significantly increases. Kellogg (2013) says simply, "Creative thinking is far too complex to be localized to just one hemisphere."

This connection between dopamine and creative mental activity has been suggested to underlie the link between the "mad genius" (Van Gogh, for example) and prolific creativity. Several documented case studies of schizophrenic painters, hypergraphic poets, and Turrets' composers clearly reveal the importance of dopamine to creativity activities (BBC Active, 1996). In these cases the torrential flow of

Figure 8.1 Vincent van Gogh's self-portrait. An unusually high level of dopamine—leading to unusual outbursts of creative activity—is consistent with the behavior of Vincent van Gogh (Van Gogh Museum Amsterdam).

dopamine drives the creator to painful levels of productivity, but sometimes questionable product. One painter, hospitalized for schizophrenia, described his mania "as not knowing when to stop, just adding more and more paint to the canvas—the result was mud."

For most of us, dopamine flows at moderate levels, and when designing an experiment or beginning a screenplay, our creative energies benefit by a structured format. For example, the structured format for an experiment requires defining of independent variables, operationalizing the levels of each by making them quantifiable. So, for example, one has observed people buy cold coffee drinks in hot weather and hot coffee drinks in cold weather. The independent variable—weather—comes in a startlingly wide range! The experimenter operationalizes by assigning or defining levels: one might choose to dichotomize saying days that are warmer than 75° F are hot and days that are cooler than 68° F are cold. This *operational definition* begins to structure the experimental design. The scientist then must select a dependent variable to measure the differences between temperatures above 75° F and below 65° F—in this case the number of hot versus cold coffee drinks bought at say the experimenter's local coffee shop. In science, the structure is mandated by mathematics—everything must be quantified. In storytelling, beginnings, middles, and endings—though not always in that order—provide structure. Other creative endeavors—painting—require collecting materials, organizing a space, preparing a canvas, and so on. (There are surely more steps in a painter's structure, but once a novice has done those they begin squishing paint from tubes and stroking brushes.) So a structured format is how to get to goal state—what sequential, sufficient, and necessary steps will lead to your creative end stage!

Cognitive psychologist Kellogg says historically creativity was defined as a product that is novel, useful, and externally validated (Hayes, 1989). If we define a screenplay as a product (it is "novel" as the writer is inventing something new, an expression of his or her own ideas into words), then we are left pondering useful; because external validation is a given—it is the reader at the production company or studio, and ultimately the audience.

Is a good story useful? Wilson argues it thus:

> The creation stories gave the members of each tribe an explanation for their existence. It made them feel loved and protected above all other tribes ... and offered meaning to the cycles of life and death. No tribe could long survive without the meaning of its existence defined

by a creation story ... The creation myth is a Darwinian device for survival. Tribal conflict, where believers on the inside were pitted against infidels on the outside, was a principal driving force that shaped biological human nature.[2]

Further arguments for storytelling's function have been laid out in Chapter 2, with the notion of stories as a learning tool for survival, and cognitive psychologist Keith Oatley's notion of story as the "mind's flight simulator."

It is safe to conclude, then, that screenwriting fits this definition of a creative mental process. So how does one get one's dopamine flowing? Cognitive scientists have found evidence that there is a process involving different states of brain activity that seem to result in creative products. Let's take these one at a time, consider the evidence for each, and then relate specifically to the screenwriting scenario.

Preparation

Preparation is the stage of studying, researching, assembling materials, including possible funding or editorial support, and preparing yourself for the product you wish to create. Research has long been an essential component of powerful, effective writing. "No matter how talented, the ignorant cannot write. Talent must be stimulated by facts and ideas. Do research. Feed your talent. Research not only wins the war on cliché, it's the key to victory over fear and its cousin, depression,"[3] advises Robert McKee. Often writers immerse themselves in the worlds they are about to create. "Write what you know" is common advice. Novelists such as James Jones (*The Thin Red Line*) and Tim O'Brien (*The Things They Carried*) wrote of war after having lived through war. John Grisham (*The Firm*) was a lawyer before writing about law. An astronomer was brought in as a consultant on the sci-fi classic *Close Encounters of the Third Kind* (1977); *Still Alice* (2014), the Oscar-winning story of a cognitive scientist developing Alzheimer's, was based on a novel written by Lisa Genova, a neuroscientist.

2. Edward O. Wilson, *The Social Conquest of Earth*. (New York: W. W. Norton, 2012), p. 8.
3. Robert McKee, *Story: Style, Structure, Substance, and the Principles of Screenwriting* (New York: HarperCollins, 1997), pp. 73–4.

Figure 8.2 *Close Encounters of the Third Kind* (1977) had a greater ring of authenticity because the filmmakers had the expert advice of an astronomer.

The more a writer has prepared, the greater likelihood the product will achieve external validation.

Incubation

While it may seem counterintuitive, the next phase, incubation, refers to taking a break—step away from the product, do something else; anything else. This stage allows the brain to refresh, to consciously engage in distraction so that the product may subconsciously incubate. Salvi and colleagues (2015) suggest visual distractions may be ideal because our attention follows our eye movements (remember Chapter 6, Shared Attention?). These researchers studied eye movements, including blinks, across preparation, incubation, and solution. Eye movements detected while participants were studying or preparing differed significantly from eye movements detected during the incubation process, when participants were consciously looking *away* from the product. During preparation, fixations—that selective type of attention that is cognitively demanding and tiring—were dominant. Fixations, even when reading (during which saccades are the natural eye movement across pages), were noted. During incubation, there was increase in eye closing or prolonged blinks, both of which relate to changes in brain activity relative to attention being internally focused. Additionally, fixations were very few, indicating participants were intentionally *not* attending to the product by letting their thoughts and attention focus on other things.

Figure 8.3 Procrastinators may take heart in scientific research indicating that walking away from one's creative work and focusing on other things—like a walk in the country—is an essential part of what is termed the *incubation* period in the creative process. This allows the unconscious mind to work. Of course, one must still return to finish it. (Chas. Worcester/Gulino Collection).

Incubation has been described by some scientists as putting it down and walking away—quite literally. Get outside the lab, or up from your computer and take a walk, take a shower, do the laundry. Get your mind and your attention on anything other than your story—this stage may be different for different individuals, some extensive products may require a two-week vacation to provide sufficient distraction for incubation. But eye movement data suggest that this stage must proceed the *illumination*, or finding the solution, to finalize the creative product.

Aha! Moment

The *Aha! Moment* (Kounios and Beeman, 2015) provides neuroimaging data that indicates this moment of insight, which happens to people in numerous situations such as finding the solution to a problem, resolution of ambiguous visual information, or even getting a joke long after it has been told, is a measurable shift in brain activity, both in the brain area where activity is located and in the type of electrical brainwave form. Illumination, then, has been described as that crucial moment when consciousness seizes upon a solution. In creative thinking, this is sometimes described as thinking outside the box, to find an original path toward breaking out of a fixed mental state.

For example, what do the words *mouse, sharp,* and *blue* have in common? This is the type of question scientists studying creativity suggest requires "outside the box" thinking. Our mindset is so fixed that we quickly associate mouse with cat, sharp with point, and blue with sky—nothing in common, right? The illumination moment, then, requires a cognitive adjustment—to discard first responses, to be more open to mind wandering than mindset. Fixation then is more than an eye movement; it is a mentally prefabricated structure that screenwriters may find inescapable. While there is no exercise that can force an Aha! insight, increasing data suggest that mindfulness meditation may soften the prefab structures and allow illumination more readily. Certainly, history is full of stories in which the problem has been overwhelming and defeat is certain until that unbidden, unsought, revelation appears and Edison has his light bulb. History also reveals that many if not most of Edison's patents were costly mistakes, in fact, exceeding his profits for that last successful light bulb (Simonton, 1997).

So then, finally, the story is told, the pages have evolved innumerous revisions, and you are ready for the final creative stage, *verification*.

Figure 8.4 The *Aha! Moment* dramatized in *Lawrence of Arabia* (1962). After a night of wandering and sitting in the wilderness, he comes to the realization about how to seize the Turkish position at Aqaba. History does not record the process by which the writers arrived at the creative decision to portray the moment this way.

And thus full circle, back to preparation, in which your final product is checked and verified, often painstaking and certainly time-consuming, this final stage of verifying that characters are full-bodied, scenes are consistent, and goals have been clearly set to reach achievement or failure as the plot dictates must conclude the creative process. It is not, of course, possible to guarantee verification in the form of a script sale or audience affirmation, but the creative process can be conducted in a way that makes such an outcome more likely.

What You Just Learned (or, Our Attempt to Load the Above Information into Your Brain's Experience Structures, a Summary of Sorts)

- *Observation*—the beginning of science and screenwriting—is our attempt to explain what we see people do (cause) and the outcomes they achieve (effect). Both science and screenwriting are storylines expressing our observations in an effort to *make sense* of our world.
- The myth of left-brain logic and right-brain poet has been dispelled by neuroimaging. We now know *creativity* is too complex for half a brain! *Dopamine* may be the neurochemical of creativity as an excess of dopamine is connected to instances of "mad genius" such as Van Gogh—since we have little knowledge of how to control our dopamine flow of creativity, it's fortunate that science and screenwriting have *structured formats* to direct our energies. A structured format provides the necessary steps toward a goal; it's not enough to see the ending, you need a clear vision of sequences and scenes to achieve a goal state.
- *Stages of creativity*, as evidenced from eye tracking and neuroimaging studies, suggest *preparation* is first—time spent researching and collecting information so the screenwriter can *write what they know*. *Incubation* follows by looking away from your script—*gaze inward* while walking outside—let your script benefit from alternative focus. *Illumination* is the stage of thinking outside the box, which can't be done on command, but if nurtured by *mind wandering*, can move your script away from stuck, or mindset. And lastly, but not by far least, *verification*, means returning full cycle to review, rewrite, to verify, that facts and character actions are consistent, that every scene tells a story.

Screenwriting Explorations: There's No Such Thing as Writer's Block

One very effective way to get writing when your body and spirit won't allow it is to sit at the computer and complain—that is, type your complaints as you think of them. Why the story doesn't work, why you're stuck, why the story, once inspiring, is something you loathe. After typing about a page of complaints, you will almost invariably find that you are now into the creative flow, solving the problems rather than being overwhelmed by them.

Another useful technique for keeping the flow of writing going across multiple writing sessions is to refrain from writing through to the end of what you have conceived clearly. That is, we often have a sense of what the content of the current scene will be as we write it, though perhaps not for the following scene. Instead of writing all the way to the end of the current scene and retiring for the night, it's best to leave some of that scene unwritten, with some notes as a guide for the next writing session. Doing it this way will make it easier for you to pick up the thread of the story in the following session, and vault forward to scenes beyond.

Yet one more simple technique you can use to keep the flow going when you feel stuck: imagine yourself as the audience watching the film and ask yourself: *What am I hoping for? What am I afraid of?*

Chapter 9

THE STRUCTURE QUESTION, OR, HOW MANY ACTS DOES IT TAKE TO SELL A SCRIPT?

It's not wise to violate rules until you know how to observe them.[1]—T. S. Eliot

The authors' hope is that the chapters in this book will empower the writer and filmmaker to navigate the various and contradictory advice he or she may receive along the journey to a screenplay or a film, by understanding the principles by which human beings perceive and process movies. How does one identify what is useful and what is not; what is profound and what is merely the current fashion? In this spirit, an investigation into some popular advice seems useful.

Syd Field popularized what came to be called the "Three Act Structure" in his 1979 book *Screenplay*. A year before this, the concept was expounded upon in *The Screenwriter's Handbook* by Virginia Oakey and Constance Nash, though it had been kicking around for years before that, often traced back to Aristotle himself in his *Poetics* in the notions of beginning, middle, and end. Field identified the acts with functions: Act I, *setup*, Act II, *confrontation*, Act III *Resolution*.

In the following decade, the work of Joseph Campbell, author of *Hero with a Thousand Faces*, became widely known through two television series about his life and work; during the 1990s, Christopher Vogler drew on Campbell's work and that of Carl G. Jung, to publish *The Writers' Journey: Mythic Structure For Writers* (1998), which laid out specific characters and specific steps in a story as follows:

---

1. T. S. Eliot, "The Art of Poetry No. 1," *The Paris Review* 21 (Spring–Summer 1959).

1. Ordinary World
2. Call to Adventure
3. Refusal of the Call
4. Meeting with the Mentor
5. Crossing the First Threshold
6. Tests, Allies, Enemies
7. Approach to the Inmost Cave
8. Ordeal
9. Reward (Seizing the Sword)
10. The Road Back
11. Resurrection
12. Return with the Elixir

Vogler maintains the three-act structure, identifying Act I as ending at step #5 and Act II ending at step #10.[2]

Such a list is a godsend for an aspiring writer because out of the almost infinite number of ways a story can be developed from the blank page, it provides a critical narrowing down of options. Plug in your ideas into this universal story pattern, and you are on your way.

The problem, of course: what about the many, many successful films that don't follow this pattern? And what about the problem of originality, of standing out from the crowd? For an aspiring screenwriter or a filmmaker to have an impact, he or she must stand out from the rest. If everyone is following the same "rules," how is this possible? Indeed, Peter Suderman, writing for *Slate* in 2013, rued that the popularity of the book *Save the Cat!* had resulted in a situation where "every movie feels the same."[3]

Even Vogler hedges things considerably.

> The Hero's Journey model is a guideline. It's not a cookbook recipe or a mathematical formula to be applied rigidly to every story. To be effective, a story doesn't have to concur with this or any other school, paradigm, or method of analysis. The ultimate measure of a story's

---

2. Christopher Vogler, *The Writer's Journey: Mythic Structure for Writers*, 3rd ed. (Studio City, CA: Michael Wiese Productions, 2007), p. 8.

3. Peter Suderman, *Save the Movie!*, Slate (2013), retrieved from http://www.slate.com/articles/arts/culturebox/2013/07/hollywood_and_blake_snyder_s_screenwriting_book_save_the_cat.html.

success or excellence is not its compliance with any established patterns, but its lasting popularity and effect on the audience.

It's possible to write good stories that don't exhibit every feature of the Hero's Journey; in fact, it's better if they don't. People love to see familiar conventions and expectations defied creatively. A story can break all the "rules" and yet still touch universal human emotions.[4]

Later, he notes, "Any element of the Hero's Journey can appear at any point in a story."[5] If we have a story paradigm that has universal appeal, but that can be switched around in any particular order, and have some pieces but not others, and that can achieve the effect of touching universal human emotions whether its principles are followed or not, perhaps it is not so useful after all in narrowing down one's options, though certainly it might provide a trigger to deeper thinking about stories.[6]

Analyzing movies according to this paradigm can be a challenge because what constitutes these various stages can be open to a great variety of interpretation, and if their order can be rearranged successfully, it may be that *every* successful film can be argued as complying with the Hero's Journey.

Someone with more certainty and fewer qualms about writers following his advice slavishly would be the late Blake Snyder, who wrote *Save the Cat!* in 2005, a book that has had broad influence. Snyder outlined his Blake Snyder Beat Sheet (BS2), confident that if you were to view six to twelve films in the genre in which you plan to write, "watch as the beats of these films are magically filled into the blanks of the BS2."[7] The numbers here refer to the page on which these beats should occur.

1. Opening Image (1)
2. Theme Stated (5)
3. Set-up (1–10)
4. Catalyst (12)
5. Debate (12–25)

---

4. Vogler, *The Writer's Journey*, p. 232.
5. Vogler, *The Writer's Journey*, p. 234.
6. Gulino has found, in twenty years of teaching, that students who know of the approach do tend to follow it more slavishly than Vogler advises, and thus it tends to limit their perceived options in developing their stories.
7. Blake Snyder, *Save the Cat* (Studio City, CA: Michael Wiese Productions, 2005), p. 96.

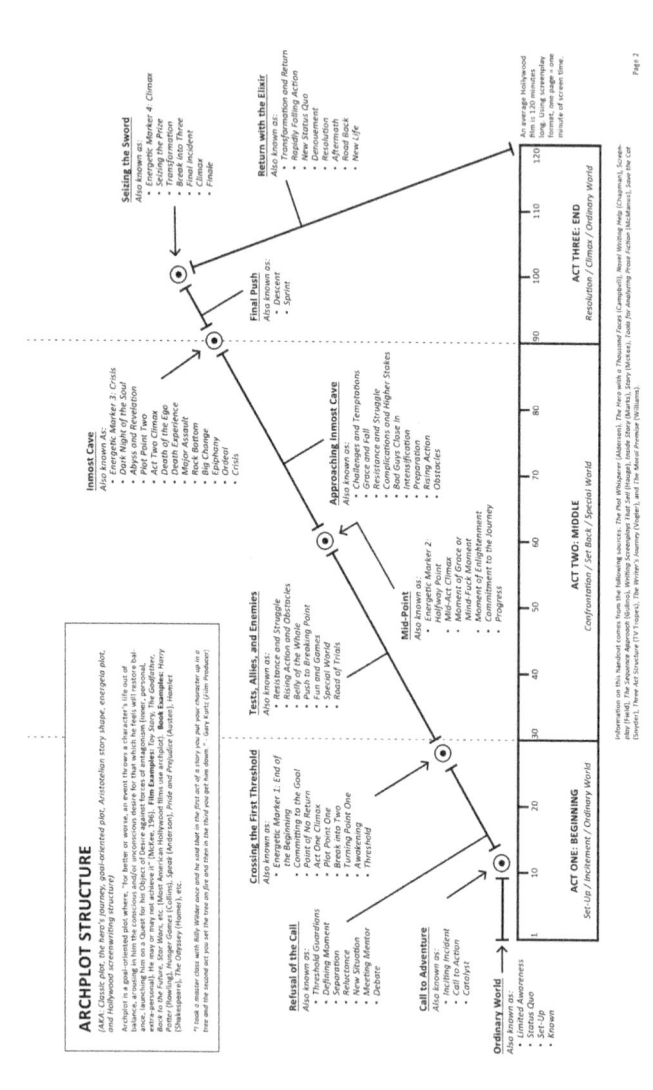

Figure 9.1 Author Ingrid Sundberg combined terminology from thirteen(!) different sources (including Gulino's sequence approach) into one amazing archplot diagram. Not for the faint of heart. Understanding the neuroscience involved can help a writer navigate between what advice is essential and what can be safely ignored. The general similarities of these models do speak to a deeper truth—structures that work with human audiences do so because they are simpatico with how human audiences perceive and process stimuli. (Ingrid Sundberg).

6. Break into Two (25)
7. B Story (30)
8. Fun and Games (30–55)
9. Midpoint (55)
10. Bad Guys Close In (55–75)
11. All Is Lost (75)
12. Dark Night of the Soul (75–85)
13. Break into Three (85)
14. Finale (85–110)
15. Final Image (110)[8]

Without going into too much detail about what these beats mean, it's safe to say that there are plenty of very successful movies that don't fit magically into these beats. *Star Wars* (1977)—see Chapter 10—is one of them.

In these two examples of screenwriting paradigm (there are plenty of others), we have rules, then we have successful filmmakers evidently breaking the rules, and the need for newcomers to distinguish themselves from others who are following the rules, and disagreements on what the rules are.

The way out of these contradictions lies in prioritizing the effect the writer/filmmaker wants to have on an audience over following particular patterns, a deeper understanding of "rules," and a recognition of which are rooted in custom and convention (schemas) and which are rooted in more basic human physiology.

Digging Deeper

Any of the above-referenced paradigms can be examined in light of how science explains our attention process—why we tune in rather than fall asleep. Should your story have three acts? Most say yes, though there are those who rail against it.[9] It actually depends on how you define the three-act structure. If it's strictly defined as a means for creating tension in the audience—that is, in the first act we learn who the main character is and what he or she wants and what the obstacles will be (thus creating

---

8. Snyder, *Save the Cat*, p. 70.
9. John Truby, *Why the 3-Act Structure Will Kill You*. Raindance (2013), retrieved online http://www.raindance.org/why-3-act-will-kill-your-writing/.

suspense born of conflict; see Chapter 7), and in the second act the main character strives to achieve the goal and overcome obstacles (the tension itself) and the third act resolves or releases that tension, then the choice of the writer becomes this: do you want to engage your audience with a central tension or not? If so, the three-act structure looks like a winning choice. In fact, it's the only choice.

The Hero's Journey? Number one, the Ordinary World, allows us to acquaint ourselves and connect emotionally with a character. Again, if one chooses to engage and audience with tension, such a connection is essential (see Chapter 2). But the first three steps also imply conflict, which is the wellspring of hypothesis or scenario-generating activity on the part of our frontal lobes, which keeps us engaged. So what is essential here is not a particular order or what these are called but that the conflict implied therein will engage an audience. Six, (Tests, Allies, Enemies), seven (Approach to the Inmost Cave), and eight (Ordeal)—all imply conflict—escalating conflict, in fact. If the conflict escalates, it provides contrast for our perceptual/cognitive system and likewise keeps us engaged (see Chapter 3). Ten (the Road Back) and eleven (Return with the Elixir) are consistent with the character arc/life lessons discussed as an evolutionary adaptation in Chapter 2. It's understandable, from a neurological viewpoint, why these pieces of a pattern would work for audience. And it's also understandable why, following Vogler's advice, one can mix and match. What matters here is the effect of these various story beats, and if you can find other beats that serve the same function, or move them chronologically and, again, preserve their effect, you can "break" the "rules" and still connect with an audience.

People don't respond to a mythic structure because of some mystical nature of myths; rather, the mythic structure hits certain aspects of our perceptual/cognitive system and resonates with it.

The Blake Snyder Beat Sheet can be seen in a similar light. Beats one (Opening Image), two (Theme Stated), and three (Set-up) serve the function of main character connection and character arc (Chapter 2). The Opening Image "gives us a moment to see the 'before' snapshot of the guy ... we are about to follow on this adventure," bookended by a Final Image (beat fifteen), which is its opposite.[10] Four and five, The Catalyst and Debate, introduce conflict and thus create suspense (see Chapter 7), which is launched in six (Break into Two). Beat eight, Midpoint, yields contrast:

---

10. Snyder, *Save the Cat*, p. 72.

[It's] either an "up" where the hero seemingly peaks (though a false peak) or a "down" when the world collapses all around the hero (though it is a false collapse), and it can only get better from here on out.[11]

Beats ten (Bad Guys Close), eleven (All Is Lost), and twelve (Dark Night of the Soul) all naturally imply conflict, and contrast (beat eleven is the opposite of the midpoint). Beat fourteen (Finale) completes the character arc (see Chapter 2): "the lessons learned are applied. It's where the character tics are mastered."[12]

As with the Hero's Journey, if you're going to write a story that employs tension as the primary means of engaging your audience, you're simply going to need certain scenes and moments that function to get us to connect with a character and set up the tension. If you want to keep your audience's attention, you're going to need to manage it through conflict and contrast. The best way to approach a theory of structure with which one is presented is to examine it in that light—is it managing audience attention, and if so, how, and are all its elements essential or variable as long as the maintenance of attention is achieved?

Breaking Those Rules

Understanding the underlying physiological and psychological reasons for certain paradigms empowers the writer to violate those paradigms and remain in command of audience attention. Yet sometimes these patterns, or paradigms, *do* become standardized because they work well. In this case, the wisdom of T. S. Eliot's observation about learning the rules before breaking them lies in understanding both the audience expectations created by schemas and the effect on the audience of violating those schemas.

As discussed in Chapter 1, schemas create expectations (schema scripts). The sight of a room containing brightly wrapped presents, streamers, balloons, paper plates, and a cake with candles on it not only suggests the schema "birthday party" but also the expectation of events to follow: arrival of guests, games, singing the song, blowing out the candles. The objects thus create an expectation.

---

11. Snyder, *Save the Cat*, p. 82.
12. Snyder, *Save the Cat*, p. 90.

When a character in a film bursts forth in song, accompanied by disembodied music, we recognize the schema *musical*. It is a pattern with which we have become familiar and which we accept without questioning the oddity of music arising from nowhere and people singing and dancing to it. Someone who wishes to create a musical will abide by that schema. Unless, of course, they are the comedy troupe Monty Python, in which case it's possible to violate the schema and get away with it (see Figure 9.1). In this case, the filmmakers actually exploited the audience's knowledge of the schema to achieve the effect they wanted: a laugh, as opposed to a song. The effect the writer/filmmaker wishes to achieve is thus the ultimate determinant of storytelling choices, not the given formula, pattern, or schema, and not what any particular manual tells you to do.

Director Alfred Hitchcock succeeded in violating an extremely well-established schema to profound effect in *Psycho* (1960). The schema: audiences were accustomed to a single-protagonist film in which the protagonist survives all the way through a movie or, more rarely, dies late in the movie. No one had ever (spoiler alert!) made a movie in which the protagonist dies less than halfway in.

Given the science of connecting to a main character, the schema of a character surviving through most or all of a movie serves the function of helping to maintain audience attention. Thus the moment the main

Figure 9.2 The King of Swamp Castle (Michael Palin) violates the schema script musical in order to get a laugh. From *Monty Python and the Holy Grail* (1975), several other examples of successful schema script violations can be found in Chapter 1.

character is dead, audience attention will be lost unless some other tool is employed. In this case, Hitchcock spent a considerable amount of screen time having the character Norman Bates clean up after what his mother had done, giving the audience a chance to connect with him. Thus the movie we thought was about a young woman on the run after stealing $40,000 is transformed almost halfway through into a movie about a young man trying to cover up the crimes of his mother. Audience attention is maintained—and the violation of the schema provides one of the most memorable jolts in cinema history.

The best way to approach screenwriting and filmmaking—and unravel the mystery of how to be distinctive yet still effective—is to think not in terms of rules but rather *effects*—what is the effect a writer/filmmaker wants to have on an audience? This allows the transformation of the writer/filmmaker from a follower (of rules) to a creator empowered to make decisions about how to affect an audience. This book provides some pathways into how audiences respond to cinema; it is up to the writer and filmmaker to use them in imaginative, innovative ways to create those memorable, perhaps indelible moments in the experience of the viewer/reader.

Chapter 10

STAR WARS, OR, HOW GEORGE DID IT

Star Wars is a history-making film with about as wide an audience as a movie can have. It managed to work over its audience's cognitive/perceptual systems not only upon release in 1977, but ever since as well: it hasn't gone out of style in forty years. Follow these simple steps and you, too, may make four billion dollars.[1]

The Opening Crawl

As discussed in Chapter 4 on the Science of Exposition, *Star Wars* begins with an information dump—a screen crawl reminiscent of serial films from the 1930s (see Figures 4.1 and 4.2). Given the fact that the human perceptual-cognitive system cannot easily absorb such information dumps, this would seem a poor strategy that might doom the film. So why wasn't it doomed? The answer to that arrives a few minutes later.

The opening dramatic scene concerns conflict immediately (Chapter 7), in this case a chase: the little space ship fleeing from the big space ship. Even though we have not yet had a chance to connect with any of the characters, suspense is immediately created around the question of whether or not that little space ship will escape—thus hooking the audience with expectation. The use of contrast is also in evidence, given the disparate sizes (see Chapter 3).

The action presented in this fight, including the cut to the inside of the small space ship, provides the answer to how Lucas got away with an information dump: the necessary information will all be repeated, and in much more (for humans) digestible form, that is, a piece at a time.[2]

---

1. Results not guaranteed. Actual amounts earned may vary appreciably.
2. It's worth noting that the filmmaker does not rely on a title card, such as "INSIDE THE SMALL SPACE SHIP" or "INSIDE THE REBEL SPACE SHIP" to identify which interior we have cut to. Instead, Lucas relies on the audience's

Figure 10.1 Darth Vader's entrance. Note the visual contrast—white versus dark. Although not in a recognizable uniform, the deferential behavior of the other troops toward him provides the audience with a clue that, through the use of top-down processing, yields our conclusion: he's the leader. *Star Wars* (1977).

One of the characters, later identified as C3PO, makes a prediction—a dangling cause—about the fate of the princess ("There'll be no escape for the princess this time.") Thus, if you missed the bit about Princess Leia in the opening title crawl, you're sure to know at the very least that there is a princess running around somewhere in the vicinity.

The action proceeds to hand-to-hand combat as the little ship is boarded. The conflict here is obvious; the outcome is in doubt only for a short time. Although the weapons involved are of a type unlike any the audience has ever encountered, their similarity to common firearms provides the schema needed for the audience to understand the action: gun battle.

The use of contrast is again in evidence with the arrival of Darth Vader, who is dressed in black while all of his soldiers are in white. Although the film does not explicitly identify him as a leader, and he does not have a uniform anything like what the audience would associate with a military leader, the filmmaker relies on other clues to signal his role, namely, the treatment he receives from the others on his side (see Figure 10.1).

propensity to piece together clues to construct a reality. In this case, an explosion is seen on the small space ship, followed by a cut that shows the occupants being thrown about. A cause-and-effect relationship between the two events is assumed by the audience, allowing ready comprehension of where the interior scene is unfolding.

The film now cuts to Princess Leia—who is not explicitly identified. Again, clues are used to convey her identity, namely, her dress and manner. This is important information repeated: once in the information dump, again in dialogue, and finally in person. She is seen inserting something into the android identified later as R2D2, then vanishes. This action—unexplained—provides a clue for the viewer's frontal lobes to store and ruminate over.

After 3CPO predicts the two androids will wind up on a junk heap (a dangling cause), the issue of the secret plans arises again when Vader questions one of the rebels. Thus, again, if one failed to comprehend the reference to these plans in the information dump (or were out getting popcorn when the said dump transpired), the information is here conveniently repeated for you. The scene ends with a *dialogue hook*, which is a form of dangling cause that triggers a cause-and-effect connection in the audience between two scenes: Vader orders his underlings to "Tear this ship apart till you have found the plans, and bring me the passengers, I want them alive!" The scramble of activity that follows is a consequence of that dangling cause.

Tension now rises around the question of whether Princess Leia can escape the search and is resolved quickly when she is captured. Soon thereafter, another brief chase occurs with a more positive outcome: the two androids escape safely from the rebel ship.

Princess Leia is now brought to Darth Vader for questioning, and a review of the information dump information once again transpires: mention again of the rebels and the secret plans, followed by more dangling causes in the form of orders from Vader to track down the plans, which, the audience knows, are with the androids.

Thus, about nine minutes into the picture we have the end of the first sequence. That sequence is unified by two elements: the battle and the pursuit/escape of the princess and the plans. The pursuit/escape provides suspense for the audience and triggers the creation of hypothetical scenarios in the audience's minds: the rebels may win, or they may lose; Princess Leia may escape, or she may not; the androids may escape, or may not (see Chapter 7). The entire action, though often following different characters in parallel, follows a cause-and-effect pattern (see Chapter 5), and is thus readily engaging to an audience that is primed to seek such patterns. It's worth noting that while there is not yet a main character to which the audience can create an emotional connection, the two androids exhibit very human and relatable qualities and suffice to generate emotional connection for the short duration of the sequence.

The end of the sequence is marked by the transition to the planet's surface, where, in order to "reset" the brains of the audience, contrast is used (see Chapter 3). The darkness of space is met by the bright sky and sand; the loud music tapers off to a quiet theme.

Used Android Salesmen

The action proceeds with an argument—conflict—between C3PO and R2D2; though we cannot understand R2D2's language, we can readily piece together the conversation from the clues provided, taking advantage of the human propensity for constructivist psychology—filling in gaps in the information provided with top-down information about how humans converse. C3PO's dialogue contains five dangling causes, including one warning ("Don't let me catch you following me for help because you won't get it") and four predictions ("I've got to rest before I fall apart," "It's much too rocky; this way is much easier," "You'll be malfunctioning within a day," and "What makes you think there are settlements over there?"). The conflict creates the tension and scenario creating; the dangling causes provide the hooks for our frontal lobes to grasp onto as we attempt to reason what is in the future.

Shortly after the two androids part ways, C3PO spots a transport and waves to it—another dangling cause. We do not see him

Figure 10.2 The initial scenes of R2D2 and C3PO are rife with conflict (see Chapter 7), contain numerous dangling causes to exploit audience propensity to seek cause and effect (see Chapter 5), and provide an emotional connection for the audience in the absence, thus far, of a protagonist (see Chapter 2). *Star Wars* (1977).

getting picked up by the transport, but the likelihood of such an outcome can be derived from our top-down understanding of such situations.

After this, contrast is again employed—bright day turns to deep twilight. R2D2 travels through rocky terrain—closing off the dangling cause—the prediction about rocks—established a few scenes previous. Various Jawas appear spying on R2D2 from the surrounding high ground. Our top-down cognitive process signals "ambush," and the outcome that transpires a short time later as the android is disabled and stowed in a transport.

Dark-to-light contrast is used in the transition to the next scene— from the interior of the transport to the bright desert landscapes as the storm troopers search for the two androids—picking up a dangling cause from the first sequence: Darth Vader's orders to send a detachment to the planet to retrieve the plans. One of the storm troopers picks up a clue: "Look, sir—Droids."

This information reinforces the pursuit/escape dynamic set up in the opening sequence and generates more hypothetical scenarios in the audience's mind: Will the storm troopers catch C3PO and R2D2, or with the androids escape? These competing hypotheses provide tension that sustains audience engagement for the rest of the sequence and beyond. Such an underlying tension is helpful in the following scene, in which Luke and his Uncle Owen purchase the two androids from the Jawas—a scene that has only minimal conflict in it. Toward the end of it, it appears that the two androids will be separated, generating that hypothetical scenario. However, with the timely failure of the chosen R2 unit, C3PO persuades Luke to take R2D2 instead.

With the resolution of the tension arising primarily from the pursuit/escape—fear that the androids will be captured by the Empire's forces (and secondarily, fear that the two will be separated), the second sequence draws to a close utilizing, again, contrast: a slow fade to black followed by the laid-back location of Luke's garage, as opposed to the imprisonment on the transport. The screenplay notes this contrast in its description: "The garage is cluttered and worn, but a friendly peaceful atmosphere permeates the low grey chamber." Thus, nineteen minutes into the film, the audience has another opportunity to reset its brain (see in Chapter 3 the discussion of valences and the timing of positive/negative information, which allows for better attention and comprehension).

The Main Character Appears

It's worth noting that one of the most successful films of all time violates an almost universal norm in filmmaking: introducing the main character early, and certainly within the first sequence. Syd Field, for example, advises, "The reader must know *who* the main character is ... within the first ten pages."[3] Blake Snyder suggests introducing the hero on page one.[4] Given that, as detailed in Chapter 2, the power of a film to engage an audience rests largely on its emotional connection to a main character, how did the film succeed without introducing its main character only after seventeen minutes had passed?

This speaks to one of the basic philosophical arguments about art in general, discussed in Chapter 9: when do you follow the rules and when do you break them? Understanding why one of the most successful films of all time succeeded despite violating the schema of an early introduction of the main character requires stepping back and figuring out the ultimate effect the filmmaker is trying to achieve, which is to *keep the audience engaged*. The use of a sympathetic protagonist with whom the audience connects emotionally is one effective, time-tested means, but it is not the only one. In this case, the filmmaker could rely on the elements discussed in the analysis of the first two sequences to maintain audience engagement till the main character could be introduced and, thereafter, carry the load.[5]

The early introduction of the main character in a narrative film has become conventional because it was tried and found to work and thus generally adopted.[6] This does not mean that alternative approaches can't

---

3. Syd Field, *Screenplay: The Foundations of Screenwriting* (New York: Random House, 2005), p. 107.

4. Blake Snyder, *Save the Cat* (Studio City, CA: Michael Weise Productions, 2005), p. 72.

5. While the *filmmaker* in this case delayed the entrance of the main character despite conventional wisdom, the screenwriter (also George Lucas) did not. The original script featured a series of scenes introducing Luke on page four, or about seven minutes into the film. The scenes did not make it into the final film.

6. The pattern was also influenced by the amount of money production companies pay stars, the preferences of the stars themselves to be seen early and often, and the expectations of audiences who want to see those stars early and often. It's noteworthy in this regard that *Star Wars* did not have a major star in its cast.

also work. Notably, another hugely successful film, *Psycho* (1960), did not introduce its main character until almost twenty-eight minutes into the picture.

Connecting to Luke

Although the tension created by the conflict in the second sequence is released in the third, with the laid-back atmosphere of Luke's garage, there remains some conflict nonetheless: Luke's inner conflict of despair at his situation, held back from an exciting life by obligations to his adopted family, as well as a minor conflict Luke has with the stubborn stains he is trying to clean up on R2D2. These are not life-or-death conflicts of the type we've seen till now, but still provide minor tension that eases us to the next major development in the story: the intersection of Luke's life and the rebel intrigue we'd witnessed in the opening. This comes in the form of the holographic image of Princess Leia. His evident attraction to her and his energetic response to mention of the rebellion are clues the audience can piece together to construct anticipation of the future of the story: Luke may well seek to participate in the rebellion, or at least to pursue Princess Leia.

This "friendly peaceful" scene accomplishes another important task: beginning the process of cementing audience emotional connection to Luke as the main character. This is realized through the clues to his personal life revealed in the conflicts: he is frustrated and longs for a more exciting life; he seems sympathetic to the rebel cause, which in turn has been portrayed sympathetically in the first sequence; he displays a youthful, naïve attraction for the Princess, who was likewise portrayed sympathetically earlier.

The following scene—dinner—completes this process of emotional connection to Luke; it reinforces his frustration with the status quo through his proposal—rejected by his uncle—to transfer to the academy a year early. Luke's subsequent gaze at the setting twin suns of the planet provides the last visual punctuation mark allowing us to gain insight into his longings and begin to assume them ourselves.

The scene also provides the audience with more clues in the form of alarmed glances between Luke's aunt and uncle when Luke describes R2D2's message and the name Ben Kenobi mentioned in it. These clues add up to *danger*, especially since the audience can see that information is being concealed from Luke (see Chapter 6 and the role of eye gaze in reading intention).

Figure 10.3 Careful blocking of the scene enables the audience to see the furtive glances between Aunt Beru and Uncle Owen, and realize that Luke does *not* see them. Humans are adapted to read the intention of others through eye gazes. One theory suggests that the contrast between the dark and light parts of the eye are an adaptation to help humans read each other's intentions by seeing where, precisely, people are looking. *Star Wars* (1977).

The sequence ends with Luke's discovery that R2D2 has escaped. His plan to pursue the android the following morning initiates the hypothesis creation in the audience, hooking it into continuing engagement in the following sequence. The onset of night and the fade to black, followed by a fade in to bright morning light, provides the contrast needed for another "reset" of the audience's brain.

The (Sand) People versus Ben Kenobi

A contrasting transition from night to bright day initiates the fourth sequence, as Uncle Owen seeks out Luke. Conflict is present even in Luke's absence: the audience is aware of Luke's whereabouts and senses the trouble he's in and Uncle Owen's comments reinforce it. The pursuit of R2D2 by Luke and C3PO is detailed in Chapter 3, where the alternative use of contrasting impressions of danger and safety sustain the attention of the audience (see Figure 3.9).

Once inside Ben's home there follows a scene heavy with exposition. As noted in Chapter 4, humans prefer their exposition—information about the circumstances of the story that is necessary for comprehension of the action—in bits and pieces. As we have seen, such exposition has been distributed in small amounts—and important information repeated—throughout the first three sequences of the film. The initial burst in the screen crawl—about the rebellion, the evil Galactic Empire, the Death Star, the secret plans—have been repeated in various ways subsequently. Further, hints and clues about Luke's father and Ben—expressed negatively by Uncle Owen—raise questions in the audience's mind and prime us for seeking answers (see Chapter 5 and the discussion of cause-and-effect reasoning).

Thus, a long scene with comparatively little conflict succeeds in being comprehensible. Ben is revealed to be very much alive (contrary to Uncle Owen's previous assertion); Luke discovers the role his father played in the Rebellion and the role Darth Vader—whom we've met—played in his demise. We also learn new things: about the Force, the Jedi Knights, and the use of the light saber. Our frontal lobes, which have absorbed information piecemeal and have a relentless tendency to create connections and seek answers, have at last been satisfied—at least for now.

The scene also presents, toward its end, a significant dangling cause (see Chapter 5). After seeing the message from Princess Leia in full for the first time, Ben attempts to convince Luke to join him, become a Jedi Knight, and join the rebellion. Luke resists and this conflict is unresolved—thus it *dangles* into the following scene.

A swift transition utilizing contrast—the bright interior of Ben's home with the darkness of space; the quiet of the Luke-Ben scene against the loud music announcing the presence of the Star Destroyer of the Empire. This scene, taking place in a room whose features and fixtures are black (as against the whiteness of Ben's place), has the same function as the Ben scene: review of information, exposition, and the creation of dangling causes. The technique used to convey this information is conflict, disagreements between the various military leaders in the room. The nature and function of the Death Star, first mentioned in the opening seconds of the film, is finally expounded upon. The power of the Force is demonstrated. The plans, which show the potential vulnerability of the Death Star, are reviewed once more. The scene ends with a dangling cause—Grand Moff Tarkin declaring "Lord Vader will provide us with the location of the Rebel fortress by the time this station is operational. We will then crush the Rebellion with one swift stroke."

This statement provides a dialogue hook into the following scene, where contrast again is used in the transition: the darkness of the Death Star conference room against the brightness of the planet's surface. Here, as if, as a consequence of Tarkin's line, the destruction of the Jawa's transport is seen. The human mind's propensity to understand events in cause-and-effect terms increases the force of this transition.

The destruction of the Jawa transport leads Luke to his home, where he discovers destruction and death. Here, the dangling cause from the Luke-Ben scene—Ben's entreaties to Luke to join the rebellion—is picked up. The last obstacle to Luke's course of action has been eliminated and the story takes a very different turn: Luke will fight for the Rebels, to avenge the death of his aunt, uncle—and father. This creates the main tension of the picture that will maintain audience attention throughout the rest of its length, in the form of two hypotheses/potential scenarios about how it could go: will he succeed in helping defeat the Empire? Or will he fail, and die trying? Thus, forty minutes in, arrives the end of the first act—defined as the moment the main tension of the story is established in the minds of the audience. This is another "violation" of the rules; many manuals, including that of Syd Field, identify twenty to thirty pages (minutes) as the best length for a first act. As with the "late" arrival of the main character, the filmmaker here utilized alternative techniques to keep the audience engaged while taking an extra long time to establish the main tension of the picture.

The sequence ends with contrast once more: the bright day of the planet and Luke's static pose, transitioning into the blackness of space and the rapid movement of space ships. The viewer's mind is reset once more, and it will need it, for the movie proper is about to begin, and with it all the emotional and cognitive demands involved in a successful and satisfying movie experience.

Mos Eisley

The fifth sequence is centered on the negotiation of an escape from the town of Mos Eisley, ending with the escape itself. It is interspersed with scenes played out in parallel aboard the Death Star. It begins by picking up a dangling cause from the previous sequence—Tarkin's declaration about finding the rebel base from Princess Leia—which in turn picks up a dangling cause from the very first sequence, in which the commander tells Vader, "She'll die before she tells you anything," and Vader replies, "Leave that to me." This involves the interrogation of Princess Leia, held prisoner. The conflict in the scene is evident, but has been set up previously by these dangling causes, such that the bulk of the conflict actually takes place offscreen. The twin potential scenarios the conflict generates in the audience's mind—she will tell or she won't—provide the tension.

Figure 10.4 Vader demonstrates the power of the Force on an underling. The film is careful to give the audience clues that it can then construct into a coherent understanding of the world in which the story takes place. Once this kind of power is established here, it comes in handy when Ben uses it to escape from the clutches of Imperial troops by using mind tricks. *Star Wars* (1977).

Contrast marks the return to the planet's surface: the darkness and blackness of the interior of the Death Star as against the brightness of the desert. Here, Luke picks up on the dangling cause from the previous sequence—Ben's entreaty that Luke become a Jedi Knight and join the rebellion—with the line, "I want to come with you to Alderaan. There's nothing here for me now. I want to learn the ways of the Force and become a Jedi like my father."[7] The action in Mos Eisley that follows is connected to this declaration in a cause-and-effect manner.

The audience is primed with an expectation of fear in the following scene, where Luke and Ben gaze down at the town of Mos Eisley and Ben says, "You will never find a more wretched hive of scum and villainy. We must be cautious." This wretched hive provides the conflict that will roll through the sequence.

After getting through an Imperial checkpoint by use of the magic powers of the Force, Luke parks the Landspeeder outside a cantina. Note the dangling causes in the dialogue that follows:

---

7. It may be argued that the end of the first act is here, since it explicitly establishes the main character's goal, which the audience knows will lead to direct conflict with Darth Vader and his forces—and thus generate the two opposite scenarios of success or failure in the audience's mind that will provide the wellspring of tension for the rest of the picture.

LUKE: Do you really think we're going to find a pilot here that'll take us to Alderaan?
BEN: Well, most of the best freighter pilots can be found here. Only watch your step. This place can be a little rough.
LUKE: I'm ready for anything.

From this exchange we determine the characters' objective (find a pilot), a prediction (Luke claims to be ready for anything), and an obstacle (the place is rough). We have already seen another obstacle: the Imperial storm troopers. Conflict thus unfolds readily in the scenes that follow, generating, again, the dueling scenarios in the audience's mind of success and failure.

Light–dark contrast is used in the transition to the bar's dark interior, where the ruffians within do indeed rough up Luke before Ben intervenes and a deal is concluded with Han Solo. That negotiation involves another dangling cause—Han bragging about the speed of his ship—and just as the tension of the negotiation is released with a successful conclusion, two new conflicts are introduced: the appearance of storm troopers looking for the androids and the appearance of Greedo as a threat to Han. The tensions are quickly resolved in a hail of gunfire in the case of Greedo and a quick exit in the case of Luke and Ben. The entire scene is well paced with positive/neutral and negative/neutral information (see Chapter 3 discussion of valences) provoking contrasting emotions in the audience.

The threat of the storm troopers returns just as Luke and companions board Han's space ship, the *Millennium Falcon*, escalating to a gun battle, intensifying the likelihood of the failure scenario in the audience's mind. The *Falcon* succeeds in blasting off, then shrugging off the interception of imperial cruisers in orbit before blasting into light speed and safety, releasing the tension that had permeated the sequence, confirming the positive hypothesis (Luke and Ben will succeed in finding a pilot for escape from Mos Eisley) and allowing the audience to reset its collective brain as the fifth sequence draws to a close.

The Journey

Contrast is used once more in the transition to the sixth sequence—in this case aurally—a burst of music. There is also a change of locale: the Death Star. Here, the story picks up a dangling cause that has lingered through several previous sequences—the interrogation of Princess Leia. In the fifth sequence, after Vader has reported to Grand Moff Tarkin that attempts to wring information from the princess have not yet been successful, Tarkin replies, "Perhaps she would respond to an alternative form of persuasion ... I think it is time we demonstrate the full power of this station"—a classic dangling cause that yields the creation of scenarios in our frontal lobes. There are plenty of clues about what Tarkin's intentions are, but none is yet confirmed.

Confirmation arrives at the start of this sequence. Conflict is employed immediately—a clash of wills between Tarkin and Leia, reinforced with indirect dialogue (see Chapter 7): Leia speaks to him metaphorically ("I should have expected to find you holding Vader's leash") and he replies ironically ("Charming to the last. You don't know how hard I found it signing the order to terminate your life!"). Soon thereafter, Leia concedes the fight and reveals the information Vader and Tarkin want—resolving that tension momentarily—while a new conflict arises immediately when Tarkin goes through with his threat—to destroy a planet using the Death Star's power—confirming audience-born speculation about Tarkin's intentions.

The switch of scene back to the *Millennium Falcon*, though happening in parallel, has a cause-and-effect aspect revealed when Ben senses a great "disturbance" in the force. The audience's propensity to search for cause-and-effect sequencing naturally (and correctly) concludes that this disturbance is the destruction of the planet Alderaan.

The remainder of the sequence is unified by the journey on the *Millennium Falcon*. The filmmaker maintains audience engagement by means of conflict aboard the ship, in two directions: Han's skepticism of Ben and his talk about the "Force," and, to a lesser extent, the conflict between the androids and Chewbacca over the board game they are playing, and finally between Luke and the "remote" while he trains with the lightsaber. The training itself is a dangling cause—preparation for a future event—which yields the dual hypotheses of success or failure in combat.

Overall, the sequence is more neutral and positive than the previous one. Because it is sandwiched between moments of high danger, the audience is capable of giving it sustained attention (see the discussion of *valences* in Chapter 2).

The tensions from these minor conflicts are resolved in turn, leading to a new, more dire conflict: the arrival in the vicinity of the now-destroyed planet Alderaan and a renewed battle with the forces of the

Empire in the form of a tractor beam pulling the *Millennium Falcon* into the Death Star. The tension from this conflict is resolved when Luke and company lose the fight against the tractor beam and are hoisted into the bowels of the massive enemy ship.

Two dangling causes emerge from the sequence: Tarkin's order to "terminate" Princess Leia after they realize she had lied about the location of the rebel base, which occurs during a brief cutaway from the *Millennium Falcon*, and Ben's reply to Han's declaration that they won't take him without a fight: "You can't win. But there are alternatives to fighting." Our frontal lobes generate competing hypotheses about whether or not Princess Leia can escape her doom, and what kind of "alternative" Ben has in mind.

Out of the Millennium Falcon and into the Garbage Room

In contrast to previous transitions between sequences, the transition from six to seven does *not* involve contrast. It's marked by the creation of a new and different tension: will Luke and the others be able to escape from the Death Star?

With the arrival of numerous storm troopers, the conflict escalates, and a negative scenario—they'll be caught—is ascendant. Clues soon emerge, though, relative to the dangling cause of the previous sequence (Ben's "alternatives to fighting"): an Imperial soldier reports to Vader that no one is on board, and that "according to the log, the crew abandoned ship right after takeoff. It must be a decoy, sir."

Since the audience knows there are people aboard, our constructivist tendencies swing into action. Gathering together the clues about Obi's comment, our knowledge of the disposition of the occupants of the *Millennium Falcon* (i.e., they *are* onboard and did *not* abandon the ship), we suspect some sort of trick. Now the audience is engaged not only on the level of conflict, but also curiosity: what is the nature of this trick—and will it work?

Soon enough, the hidden compartments aboard the ship are revealed, along with Luke and the others; this is followed soon afterward by the abduction and disposal of the scanning crew and two storm troopers, and the uniform switch, and the nature of Ben's plan is exposed, along with the temporary release of tension: they succeed in overcoming the threat posed by the search. Conflict and dangling causes are instilled even in this episode; after emerging from their hiding places, this exchange takes place:

> **HAN:** This is ridiculous. Even if I could take off, I'd never get past the tractor beam.
> **BEN:** Leave that to me!
> **HAN:** Damn fool. I knew that you were going to say that!

Both express thoughts about the future, but Han is deeply skeptical—and critical—of Ben.

Luke and company use their disguises—and blasters—to seize control of a small command room, where Han's skepticism provides yet more grist for the conflict mill.

> **HAN:** Where did you dig up that old fossil?
> **LUKE:** Ben is a great man.
> **HAN:** Yeah, great at getting us into trouble.
> **LUKE:** I didn't hear you give any ideas . . .
> **HAN:** Well, anything would be better than just hanging around waiting for him to pick us up . . .

The personal conflict between Luke and Han for most of the rest of the movie—over such issues such as Han's loyalty, his skepticism of the Force, and rivalry for Princess Leia—laces the scenes that follow even as larger conflicts loom on multiple levels.

In the command room, two dangling causes established previously are picked up: Ben determines the means of shutting down the tractor beam, thus allowing the *Millennium Falcon* to escape, and Princess Leia, awaiting execution, is located. Ben sets off to shut down the tractor beam while Luke and Han set off to rescue the princess—an activity that unifies the remainder of the sequence.

In developing a plan to sneak into the cell block where Princess Leia is being held, Luke actually relies on a bit of constructivist psychology himself: in response to Han's question: "What's your plan?" Luke picks up a pair of binders (handcuffs) and attempts to put them on Chewbacca. The wookiee raises a fuss, but Han smiles and says, "Don't worry, Chewie. I think I know what he has in mind."

Han pieces together the clues and the situation and realizes what Luke is up to; the audience remains in the dark but its frontal lobes are engaged in trying to figure out what Han has figured out. Soon enough, we see Luke and Han, disguised as storm troopers, "escorting" a captured wookiee through the corridors of the Death Star, and part of their plan is revealed; the rest is disclosed when they arrive at the detention center and pretend that Chewbacca has overpowered them, leading to a firefight in which all the guards are killed.

This firefight provides a brief but spectacular contrast to the subdued conflicts in the previous several scenes—a wake-up call to our sensations that allow a quick reset of our attention. After the guards are defeated (resolving that tension), Han promises another: "Luke! We're going to have company!" Soon thereafter, the tension surrounding the rescue of the princess, and the two competing potential scenarios (they'll succeed or they won't), is released when Luke locates her and frees her from the cell.

A cutaway to a quieter setting—the conference room—provides a contrast to the noise and action of the detention center. Here, Vader tells Tarkin that Obi Wan (Ben) is onboard the ship. Tarkin tells him he must not escape the ship, to which Vader replies with a dangling cause: "Escape is not his plan. I must face him alone."

Back in the detention center, the dangling cause of the imminent arrival of "company" is picked up as storm troopers start blasting through the door. The all-out battle—with its attendant rapid action, flashes of light, and sound—escalates till the three manage to escape through an air chute, resolving the tension surrounding their escape from the detention center and bringing the sequence to an end. Just before their escape, Han manifests an inner conflict that supplements the external conflict of all-out physical battle when he says, of Princess Leia, "Wonderful girl! Either I'm going to kill her or I'm beginning to like her." Even the phrase "Wonderful girl!" is indirect—Han means the opposite (see Chapter 7).

Escape from the Garbage Room

The transition to the seventh sequence involves contrast once more—the blaster battle, with its high tension and sight and sound, to the release of tension (Luke and company successfully escape) and the quiet of the garbage room. Again, a chance for the brain to reset.

There remains the underlying tension surrounding the question of escaping the Death Star in the *Millennium Falcon* to maintain audience attention and the more particular question of escaping from the garbage room (which Han tries to effect immediately—and unsuccessfully—with his blaster against the door). To these tensions is added a new one—some kind of serpent creature in the waters of the garbage room that poses an immediate threat. All of these tensions, of course, arise from conflicts the characters face that yield competing scenarios in the audience's mind for the outcomes, and keep our attention focused on seeking answers (see Chapter 5).

The tension—and audience's fear—rises when Luke is taken underwater by the serpent creature and seems to drown. In fact, the filmmaker presents clues that suggest the worst has indeed happened: a long pause, still waters, and no sign of Luke. Or, as the screenplay put it: "Then everything is deathly quiet. Han and Leia give each other a worried look as Chewbacca howls in the corner."

Our constructivist tendencies immediately put these clues together and hypothesize what, apparently, Han and Leia are hypothesizing: that Luke is dead. As it turns out, though, the filmmaker is simply doing what good filmmakers often do: setting up a surprise twist by counting on the audience's constructivist tendencies—and his control over the clues provided—to lead us to the wrong conclusion.

Luke does reappear—mysteriously unharmed ("I don't know, it just let go of me and disappeared ..."). This may seem a bit of a cheat and therefore disappointing—the problem posed by the filmmaker solves

Figure 10.5 The garbage room scene is the culmination of a series of increasingly difficult situations Luke and company find themselves in, each of which ratchets up audience tension by relying on our frontal lobes to spin out conflicting alternative scenarios: get discovered by stormtroopers or maintain secrecy, then when they are found out, get shot by a blaster or get away, and finally, when in the garbage room—get crushed or escape. The positive outcome—escape—happens in a way that is carefully set up earlier. *Star Wars* (1977).

itself—but there are two mitigating facts in its favor. One is the existence of the Force—it has been discussed in various ways throughout most of the film and references to it by Ben and Vader have become more frequent. Could this be a manifestation of that? The other is that a new conflict arises even as Luke emerges from his doom: the closing in of the walls. The two readily generated hypotheses are obvious: they'll be crushed or they'll escape. Thus the brief relief from Luke emerging alive from the water is contrasted immediately to the escalating danger—and noise (both shouting and the sound of material being crushed).

There is yet another layer of conflict and tension that is integral to the "trash compactor" scene above: the discovery and escape of R2D2 and C3PO from the command room, a series of scenes that are intercut with the garbage room. In fact, on one level the danger posed by the potential capture of the two androids is greater than that posed by the death of Luke, Han, and Leia, because R2D2 has the secret plans that can preserve the Rebellion.

As the walls of the garbage room close in, C3PO, in the command room, succeeds in bluffing his way past a guard and he and R2D2 move to a space where he is able to communicate with Luke. Alerted to Luke's dilemma, R2D2 taps into the computer system to halt the movement of the walls, saving the lives of Luke and company.

Contrivance: A Digression

Most moviegoers have had the experience of watching a film in which the main character gets into some inextricable dilemma, then, through some unconvincing means, gets out of it, leading to a groan or just general disappointment—or the feeling of being cheated. The traditional term for such a "cheat" is *deus ex machina*—"God from a machine." The concept originated in classical Greek theater, and refers to the practice of having a god—lowered onto the stage via a crane—arriving just in time to solve the characters' problems (see Figure 9.2). Theorists have taken a generally dim view of such a practice since Aristotle, who noted in his *Poetics*, "It is therefore evident that the unraveling of the plot, no less than the complication, must arise out of the plot itself, it must not be brought about by the Deus ex Machina."[8] That is, the means of escape from a dilemma should be

---

8. Aristotle, *Poetics,* p. 55.

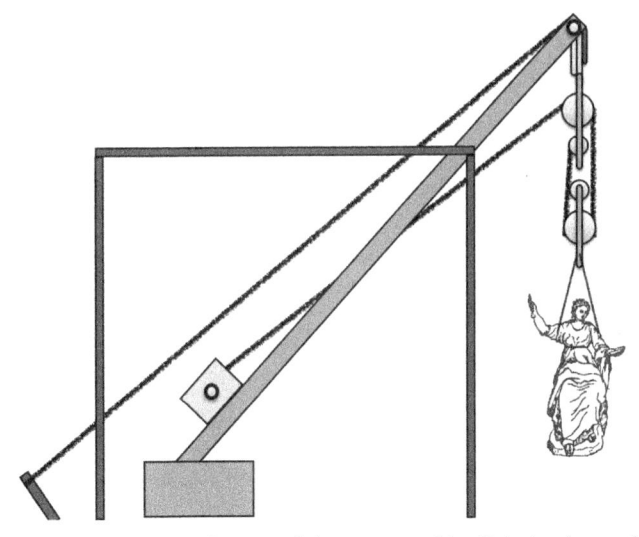

Figure 10.6 *Deus ex machina*: God (or is it a goddess?) being lowered on a machine. Don't try this at home (or in your screenplay). (Gulino).

built into the fabric of the story itself, not introduced in some all-too-convenient manner.

The screenplay for *Star Wars* evinces much care Lucas took in working out its many chases and escapes in ways that are inventive and convincing. In the garbage room sequence, it's worth noting that while Luke, Han, and Leia are unable to solve their dilemma without help from the outside, the positive outcome is satisfying because the elements needed for their escape have been put in place ahead of time by the filmmaker (or, in Aristotle's terms, they arise "from the plot itself"). These involve the remote comlink by which Luke is able to communicate with C3PO, and R2D2's ability to tap into the Death Star's computer system and manipulate it. Thus the filmmaker has provided the clues by which a perceptive viewer might well construct an escape route, even if the specific means of escape come as a surprise.

Examples of the careful setup of escape routes are everywhere in the screenplay. In the Mos Eisley sequence, when imperial storm troopers stop Luke's vehicle and question him about the androids, the danger of capture is high. However, Ben uses the Force to exert mind control over the troopers to get through (he later uses a similar trick to escape from the watchful eye of another group of storm troopers aboard the Death Star, described later). This might seem like a cheat, but it's carefully set up earlier when Ben first talks to Luke about the power of the Force, and we later see the power of the Force demonstrated by Vader when he uses it to strangle an underling in the Death Star. In a similar vein, Ben's use of the lightsaber to neutralize an alien in the bar in Mos Eisley occurs only after the lightsaber had been introduced and discussed. In the final, climactic battle, Luke turns off his computer and uses the Force to help guide his aim with the torpedoes—an approach to combat introduced earlier when Luke tries to use the Force to guide him in blindly sparring with a "remote" aboard the *Millennium Falcon*. Luke's use of a nylon cable with a grappling hook—which he uses to effect his and Leia's escape from the retracted bridge in the Death Star—may seem convenient or contrived, since we've not seen it till the moment it's needed. However, Luke gets it from a utility belt he's wearing, something that was part of the Imperial storm trooper uniform he'd just recently worn. Thus the escape is, again, something woven into the fabric of the world the filmmaker created.

This kind of care by the filmmaker—thinking through and establishing a robust world with many clues that the audience can observe for later use—doubtless contributes to the durable appeal of the film. A much more pedestrian solution to the Garbage Room escape, for example, might be that Luke just happens to find an escape hatch and that he's able to open, just in time. Or perhaps there happens to be a really strong piece of metal in the garbage that stops the compactor from working. Maybe Luke and Han put their arms against the closing walls and really exert themselves, and their combined strength stops them.

Many films are littered with these kinds of less-than-satisfying escapes from danger. In *Gravity* (2013), the main character escapes certain death because a ghost appears and tells her which button to push; in *Captain America: Winter Soldier* (2014), the title character finds himself in an elevator surrounded by brawny bad guys and gets out because, apparently, he's just a better fighter. George Lucas himself in a later work was not immune. At one point in *The Phantom Menace* (1999), two Jedi Knights—a youthful Obi Wan and his mentor Qui-Gon—wait in a conference room when poison gas is pumped in. Their escape route: they just hold their breath. Problem solved. When the room is opened, the two confront dozens of battle droids. The solution: they cut them all down with lightsabers. Problem solved again.

Such easy and convenient solutions to dilemmas tend to undermine any fear the audience might have for the fate of the characters, because a schema begins to emerge: with little effort, the characters will be able to survive everything, so there's no need to worry. This, in turn, reduces the emotional intensity of the experience.

Escape from the Death Star

Contrast in sound—the loud cheering of Luke and company in the garbage room against the quiet of the corridors outside—marks the transition from the eighth to the ninth sequence. The dangling cause from sequence seven—Ben telling the others he will disable the tractor beam—is picked up immediately as Ben arrives at the tractor beam controls and disables it. He accomplishes this despite a new conflict—the arrival of storm troopers nearby, creating tension: will he be caught or will he succeed? The positive scenario is confirmed when he uses the Force to trick the storm troopers into looking away—another use of the Force that has been woven into the fabric of the world the filmmaker created.

Meanwhile, the personal conflict between Leia and Han continues as they and Luke make their way within sight of the *Millennium Falcon*, picking up the dangling cause of their desire to escape from it. Their journey from here to the ship itself provides several scenes of heightened conflict: Han getting the upper hand on a group of storm troopers— releasing tension—then finding himself being chased by them, creating heightened fear and tension once more. Meanwhile, Luke gets Leia in trouble when the two are trapped on a ledge, increasing the likelihood of a negative scenario in the audience's mind, and then leads them to safety through heroic acrobatics, releasing *that* tension.

Brief interludes of Ben quietly sneaking around the Death Star provide an aural contrast to the loud, visually dazzling battle scenes with the storm troopers. As Ben makes his way to near the *Millennium Falcon*, he encounters Vader, picking up on a dangling cause from the seventh sequence in which Vader predicted that Ben would want to meet him alone. This conflict escalates into a lightsaber fight, distracting the storm troopers who are guarding the space ship and allowing Luke and the others to make their way onboard, after Han says, "Just hope the old man got the tractor beam out of commission," picking up on the earlier dangling cause (Ben's mission to disable it) while thrusting it into a future expectation.

The departure of the storm troopers would seem a convenient coincidence, but because the Ben–Vader lightsaber fight has already been established in the vicinity, it follows a readily acceptable cause-and-effect sequencing (see Chapter 5).

The tension arising from the conflict between Ben and Vader is resolved in a sudden and unexpected way—Ben acquiescing to his own death—confirming the *negative* potential scenario created by the conflict.[9] Luke overcomes his shock and makes it onto the space ship with the others, where Han takes the controls and reminds us once more of a critical dangling cause: "I hope the old man got that tractor beam out of commission, or this is going to be a real short trip."

The *Millennium Falcon* succeeds in blasting away from the Death Star, providing a momentary resolution to the conflict surrounding the question of escape. Contrast in visual (action vs. inaction) and sound (loud vs. quiet) reinforce the impression that the effort has been successful. In this moment, Luke is left to digest emotionally the loss of his mentor.

The quietude does not last long: Han reports the presence of Imperial sentry ships, and the conflict, on a life-and-death scale, ramps up once more as he and Luke fend off the attackers. The twin potential scenarios—victory and defeat—are generated by this conflict, and during the battle, the likely outcome veers from one to the other until all four enemy TIE fighters are destroyed, at which time the tension surrounding the escape of the *Millennium Falcon* is at last released as it blasts away at light speed. The sequence ends with an ominous dangling cause: a cut back to the Death Star where Tarkin says, "You're sure the homing beacon is secure aboard their ship? I'm taking an awful risk, Vader. This had better work."

Getting Ready

The tenth sequence is unified by scenes of preparation—which prime the audience—for the final battle against the Death Star. It begins with a conversation between Han and Leia, in which conflict is immediately

---

9. Such a profoundly negative outcome to a conflict is rare in series, where recurring characters are the norm. The feature form (and the limited series) provides greater flexibility in this regard, yielding an intensely rich emotional experience otherwise impossible if the audience can always be assured the principle characters will make it through. In effect, a feature offers an audience an "anything can happen" experience.

employed: Han bragging about the successful escape, Leia arguing that imperial forces *let* them escape and are likely tracking them—a suspicion the audience already knows is true. A dangling cause follows: Leia explaining to Han that R2D2 contains the technical readouts of the Death Star and adding, "I only hope that when the data is analyzed, a weakness can be found." Because the audience has made an emotional connection with her, the hope she expresses is our own. But in uttering it, she creates a new conflict with Han, who insists he's done with the whole thing and simply wants his money. Leia leaves the cockpit and Luke takes her place, and a new conflict erupts: rivalry between Luke and Han for Leia, which sustains audience engagement till the *Millennium Falcon* arrives at the rebel base.

At this point, the work of priming the audience for the climactic battle begins in earnest. The conflict implied in the impending attack on the Death Star gets the audience's frontal lobes working to generate two alternative possible scenarios: success or failure. The rest of the sequence is dedicated to favoring the latter—increasing the fear in the audience. The fighter pilots are told they must strike a target two meters in diameter. This inspires skepticism from Han, who is listening in, and from a fighter pilot named Wedge Antilles, who comments, "That's impossible, even for a computer." Luke pushes back by declaring, "It's not impossible. I used to bull's-eye womp rats in my T-sixteen back home. They're not much bigger than two meters."[10] But the scene quickly switches to the Death Star, which is revealed to be thirty minutes away from firing on the rebel base, posing a new and severe danger.[11] A dangling cause

---

10. Luke's flying and shooting prowess, which become of central and pivotal importance in the climactic moments of the picture, may seem like a bit of a cheat here (see the discussion above about *deus ex machina*) because to this point we have never seen Luke fly a fighter, though we *have* seen him do some shooting, with blasters and in fighting off enemy ships in the *Millennium Falcon*. The original screenplay actually *did* attempt to set up his flying ability. In an early scene that did not make it into the film, Luke has a conversation with an old friend and fighter pilot, Biggs Darklighter, who makes his return in the final two sequences. In the conversation Luke describes a dogfight he had while piloting a "skyhopper," thus setting up his piloting prowess and declaration about bull's-eying womp rats.

11. The reference to thirty minute is known as a *deadline*, and it is a useful tool for screenwriters to create anticipation, because audiences will pick it up as a clue to the time frame in which action must take place.

Figure 10.7 Han tells Luke the attack on the Death Star is "suicide." The two alternative scenarios the assault generates in the audience's frontal lobes—success against the Death Star or failure—are amplified in the scenes before the battle, with emphasis on the negative scenario. This enhances through contrast the ultimate triumph of Luke and the Rebellion. *Star Wars* (1977).

soon follows: Vader telling Tarkin, "This will be a day long remembered. It has seen the end of Kenobi and it will soon see the end of the Rebellion." The negative outcome, constructed in the minds of the audience from the clues presented, looms more menacingly.

Han pushes the menace further in the next scene, in which he declines to participate in the attack with the words, "What good's a reward if you ain't around to use it? Besides, attacking that battle station ain't my idea of courage. It's more like suicide." This is followed by some contrasting dangling causes. Luke encounters his old friend Biggs, who tells him, "You'll tell me your stories when we come back," and "they'll never stop us." This follows a remark by Red Leader to Luke: "You'll do all right." The sequence ends with a dangling cause from the disembodied voice of Ben: "Luke, the Force will be with you."

The Battle

The eleventh sequence begins with the launch of the rebel fighters into battle. Contrast is used here—the relative quiet of the fighter hangar to the battle with its crescendo of engine noises, blasters, shouting, and loud music. The conflict is obvious: the Empire and the Death Star against Luke and the rebels. The competing scenarios of success or failure are well established previously. The sequence plays out as individual conflicts between the rebel pilots and enemy artillery and fighters.

Despite the almost continuous action, there is the use of contrast—in both visual/aural elements and tension/release—interspersed throughout the battle. There are occasional cutaways to the interior of the Death Star, where Tarkin follows the course of the battle, and the rebel base; these locations offer relatively quiet interludes that allow a brief "reset" of the audience's brain. Then there are the tension-and-release patterns: Luke fires at the surface of the Death Star and seems to be headed for a crash with a fireball (increasing tension), then pulls through successfully (tension released). Biggs gets an enemy fighter on his tail (increasing tension); Luke shoots it down (tension released). Luke winds up being pursued (increasing tension); Wedge shoots the pursuer down (tension released). Initial attack run nears the target (raising hope); Vader shoots all three down (increasing fear). Second attack yields a direct hit (raising hope); it "impacts on the surface" and fails (increasing fear). Throughout these scenes, we are reminded occasionally of the deadline by way of a countdown—at which point the rebel base will be destroyed. This, of course, serves to increase the tension.

With Luke's run, the tension is wound up to the highest pitch: music, action, rapid cutting, loss of Biggs and R2D2 to Vader's guns, Luke all alone with Vader closing in. Release from the tension comes at last with the timely return of Han to disrupt menacing enemy fighters, clearing the way for Luke to fire his torpedoes under the guidance of the Force and destroy the Death Star.

Figure 10.8 Epilogue of triumph. Periodically throughout the film, contrast is used to "reset" the audience's brain and keep it fresh for the next segment of the story, when new tensions would arise. With all conflicts resolved at the end, and thus all tensions released, the audience is given an entire epilogue to reset its brains before heading out to the parking lot in their leisure suits to listen to eight-track tapes en route to the disco. *Star Wars* (1977).

A brief epilogue follows, allowing the audience to reset its brains one more time before returning to the "real world." During its three minutes, there is only the slightest bit of tension: whether or not R2D2 can be repaired, and even this is minimized with a promising dangling cause: Luke telling C3PO: "He'll be all right." This dangling cause is closed off near the end of the last scene of celebration, enhancing the sense of celebration and release from the tension the audience's brains had experienced from the opening screen crawl.

Chapter 11

EPILOGUE, OR, GO FORTH AND CREATE

There once was a man with a very long beard. One day someone asked him a question: when you sleep at night, do you sleep with your beard on top of the blankets or underneath them? The man could give no answer: he had no idea, and had never even thought about it before. However, from that day on, he could never sleep, because he couldn't get the question out of his mind, and would attempt to stay up every night to find out what the answer was.

Scientists have a term for summing up a learning experience: *metacognition*. This consists of finding connections between new information and what has always been known, and the final sorting into comprehensible categories the now blended, refined, refreshed knowledge one has gained.

Anyone reading this far is now capable of undertaking metacognition, but most are presumably more interested in success in writing a screenplay or making a film than in continuing any scientific inquiry. The process of tying it all together, or thinking about thinking, eventually exhausts our cognitive resources. So how does one proceed from here?

Frank Daniel used to tell the above-quoted story of the old man with a beard to illustrate the dilemma. Once you've got these concepts in your mind, it can be impossible to dislodge them, indeed impossible to see screenwriting in particular and cinema in general the way you did before. To put it more scientifically, your neural pathways may be clogged with ideas and the strategies you've explored in reading this book. However, you need action to become practiced and as you've learned in this book, neurons that get into action are bound to become experts.

Some strategies for getting your neurons in action were suggested at the end of Chapter 8. It may also be useful to review the various screenwriting exercises and cognitive experiments contained at the end of the chapters—that is, play around a bit creatively. The key for going forth and creating is to temporarily forget the many lessons learned in this volume, get emotionally engaged with your creative impulses (experiment with how best to generate this; often listening to music can help), and pour it out on the page without attempting to analyze it in light of narrative concepts.

Once the screenplay exists in draft form, or the film in a rough cut, the various lessons contained herein can come in handy as diagnostic tools, used to identify the cause of any problems perceived in the work, and bring an initial creative impulse to its full potential.

Good luck.

REFERENCES

Adornetti, I. (2016). "On the Phylogenesis of Executive Functions and Their Connection with Language Evolution," *Frontiers in Psychology,* 7: 14–26. doi:10.3389/fpsyg.2016.01426.

Aristotle (1902). *Poetics.* Translated by S. H. Butcher. London: Macmillan.

Asutay, E. and Vastifjall, D. (2015). "Negative Emotion Provides Cues for Orienting Auditory Spatial Attention." *Frontiers in Psychology,* 6: 618. http://dx.doi.org/10.3389/fpsyg.2015.00618.

Badt, K. L. (2015). "A Dialogue with Neuroscientist Jaak Pankseep on the SEEKING System: Breaking the Divide between Emotion and Cognition in Film Studies." *Projections* 9 (1): 66–79.

BBC Active (1996). *Touched by Genius: A Neurological Look at Creativity.* Princeton, NJ: Films for the Humanities and Sciences.

Bolt, Robert and Wilson, Michael (1962). In *Lawrence of Arabia,* directed by David Lean. Culver City, CA: Columbia Pictures, pp. 9, 127.

Bordwell, D. (2007). *Narration in the Fiction Film.* Madison: University of Wisconsin Press.

Bordwell, D., and Thompson, K. (2006). *Film Art: An Introduction,* 1st ed. NewYork: McGraw-Hill.

Bordwell, D., Thompson, K., and Staiger J. (1985). *The Classical Hollywood Cinema: Film Style & Mode of Production to 1960.* New York: Columbia University Press.

Boyd, B. (2005). "Evolutionary Theories of Art." In *The Literary Animal: Evolution and the Nature of Narrative,* edited by Jonathan Gottschall and David Sloan Wilson. Evanston, IL: Northwestern University Press.

Brunetiere, Ferdinand (1903). *Etudes Critiques,* vol. VII. Paris: Librairie Hachette et Cie.

Carroll, N., and Seeley, W. P. (2013). "Cognitivism, Psychology, and Neuroscience: Movies as Attentional Engines." In *Psychocinematics: Exploring Cognition at the Movies,* edited by Arthur P. Shimamura, pp. 53–75. Oxford: Oxford University Press.

Christoforou, C., Christou-Champi, S., Constantinidou, F., and Theodorou, M. (2015). "From the Eyes and the Heart: A Novel Eye-Gaze Metric That Predicts Video Preferences of a Large Audience." *Frontiers in Psychology,* 6 (579): 1–11. http://journal.frontiersin.org/article/10.3389/fpsyg.2015.00579. doi: 10.3889/fpsyg.2015.00579.

Cohen, A. J. (2013). Film Music and the Unfolding Narrative. In *Language, Music and the Brain,* edited by M. A. Arbib, pp. 173–201. Cambridge, MA: MIT Press.

Cutting, James E., DeLong, Jordan E., and Nothelfer, Christine E. (2009). "Attention and the Evolution of Hollywood Film," *Psychological Science*, 21 (3): 432–9, doi:10.1177/0956797610361679.

Eliot, T. S. (1959). "The Art of Poetry No. 1." *Paris Review* 21 (Spring–Summer).

Field, Syd (2005). *Screenplay: The Foundations of Screenwriting*. New York: Random House.

Freytag, Gustav (1900). *Technique of the Drama: An Exposition of Dramatic Composition and Art*, translated by E. J. MacEwan. Chicago: Scott, Foresman.

Gottschall, Jonathan (2012). *The Storytelling Animal*. Boston, MA: Houghton Mifflin Harcourt.

Graesser, A., Singer, M., and Trabasso, T. (1994). "Constructing Inferences during Narrative Text Comprehension." *Psychological Review*, 101: 371–95.

Gregory, R. L. (1997). *Eye and Brain: The Psychology of Seeing*. 5th ed. Oxford: Oxford University Press.

Gulino, P. J. (2004). *Screenwriting: The Sequence Approach*. New York: Bloomsbury.

Hayes, J. R. (1989). *The Complete Problem Solver*. 2nd ed. Hillsdale, NJ: Lawrence Erlbaum.

Howard, David, and Edward Mabley (1995). *The Tools of Screenwriting*. New York: St. Martin's Griffin.

James, William (1890/1981). "Principles of Psychology." In *Sensation and Perception*, edited by E. B. Goldstein (2007), 8th ed. Belmont, CA: Cengage Learning.

Kellogg, R. T. (2013). *Fundamentals of Cognitive Psychology*. Los Angeles, CA: Sage Publications.

Kounios, J., and Beeman, M. (2009). "The *Aha!* Moment: The Cognitive Neuroscience of Insight." *Current Directions in Psychological Science*, 18 (4): 210–16.

Lasseter, J. et al. (1995) *Toy Story*, directed by John Lasseter. Emoryville, CA: Pixar Animation Studios and Burbank, CA: Walt Disney Pictures, p. 36.

Martin, D. U., Perry, C., and Kaufman, J. H. (2016). "An Eye on Animacy and Intention." *Frontiers in Psychology*, 7: 829.

McKee, Robert (1997). *Story: Style, Structure, Substance, and the Principles of Screenwriting*. New York: HarperCollins.

Michael, J. (2016). "What Are Shared Emotions (for)?" *Frontiers in Psychology*, 7: 412.

Nettle, D. (2005). "What Happens in Hamlet?" In *The Literary Animal: Evolution and the Nature of Narrative*, edited by J. Gottschall. and D. S. Wilson. Evanston, IL: Northwestern University Press.

Oakey, Virginia and Constance Nash (1978). *The Screenwriter's Handbook*. New York: HarperCollins.

Pincus, David (2010). "And the Oscar Goes to ... Our Brains?" *Psychology Today*. https://www.psychologytoday.com/blog/the-chaotic-life/201003/and-the-oscar-goes-toour-brains.

Rapp, D. N., and Gerrig, R. (2002). "Readers' Reality-Driven and Plot-Driven Analyses in Narrative Comprehension." *Memory & Cognition*, 20 (5): 779–88.

Salvi, C., Bricolo, E., Franconeri, S. L., Kounios, J., and Beeman, M. (2015). "Sudden Insight Is Associated with Shutting Out Visual Inputs." *Psychonomic Bulletin Review*, 22: 1814–19.

Simonton, D. K. (1997). "Creative Productivity: A Predictive and Explanatory Model of Career Trajectories and Landmarks." *Psychological Review*, 104: 66–89.

Smith, N. (2003). "Dissociation and Modularity: Reflections on Language and Mind." In *Mind, Brain and Language*, edited by M. Banich and M. Mack, pp. 87–111. Mahwah, NJ: Lawrence Erlbaum.

Snyder, Blake (2005). *Save the Cat*. Studio City, CA: Michael Weise Productions.

Sorkin, Aaron (2010). *The Social Network*, directed by David Fincher. Culver City, CA: Columbia Pictures.

Storm, B. C., and Patel, T. N. (2014). "Forgetting as a Consequence and Enabler of Creative Thinking." *Journal of Experimental Psychology: Learning, Memory, and Cognition*, 40 (6): 1594–609.

Suderman, Peter (2013), *Save the Movie!*, Slate, retrieved from http://www.slate.com/articles/arts/culturebox/2013/07/hollywood_and_blake_snyder_s_screenwriting_book_save_the_cat.html.

Thomson-Jones, K. J. (2013). "Sensing Motion in Movies." In *Psychocinematics: Exploring Cognition at the Movies*, edited by Arthur P. Shimamura, pp. 115–32. Oxford: Oxford University Press.

Tognoli E. and Kelso J. A. S. (2014). "Enlarging the Scope: Grasping Brain Complexity." *Frontiers in Systems Neuroscience*, 8: 122.

Tomasello, M., Hare, B., Lehmann, H., and Call, J. (2007). "Reliance on Head versus Eyes in the Gaze Following of Great Apes and Human Infants: The Cooperative Eye Hypothesis." *J. Hum. Evol.* 52: 314–20. doi: 10.1016/j.jhevol.2006.10.001.

Truby, John (2013). *Why the 3-Act Structure Will Kill You*. Raindance, retrieved online http://www.raindance.org/why-3-act-will-kill-your-writing/.

Vallet, G. T., Brunel, L., Riou, B., and Vermeulen, N. (2016). "Dynamics of Sensorimotor Interactions in Embodied Cognition." *Frontiers in Psychology*, 6 (1929). http://dx.doi.org/10.3389/fpsyg.2016.01929.

Vogler, Christopher (2007). *The Writer's Journey: Mythic Structure for Writers*, 3rd ed. Studio City, CA: Michael Wiese Productions.

Warren, R. M. (1970). "Perceptual Restoration of Missing Speech Sounds." *Science*, 167: 392–3.

Wilder, Billy, and Chandler, Raymond (1944). *Double Indemnity*, directed by Billy Wilder, Los Angeles, CA: Paramount Pictures, pp. 11–12.

Wilson, Edward O. (2012). *The Social Conquest of Earth*. New York: W. W. Norton.

INDEX

Adam's Rib (1949) 11–14
Aristotle 23, 29, 33, 65, 148–9
attention 79
  cost of (attention) 89
  divided 80, 90
  eye gaze 82, 90
  movement 81, 90
  selective 80, 90
  shared 81
Avatar (2009) 16, 95

blurring 23–4, 33
Breaking Bad (2008–2013) 20, 25, 28, 38, 42, 44
Bullets Over Broadway (1994) 67

CAM-WN model 7 (illustration) 22, 40, 74
  Cloud 74
Captain America: Winter Soldier (2014) 150
cause and effect 65–77
  dangling cause, 72 (defined) 73, 76, 132–5, 139–46, 151–4
  goal state 74, 82
  motives 73
  physical cause and effect 70
character arc 29–31, 34, 126–7
Close Encounters of the Third Kind (1977) 114–15
cones 80
conflict 93–110
  emotion 100
  fractual 95
  human cognition 96–7
  human perception 96
  indirect 106, 108
  internal 104
  Muller-Lyer illusion 99
  top-down vs bottom-up 99
  verbal 101
constructivist psychology (constructivism) 9, 55, 60, 63, 134, 145, 147
  bottom-up process 5, 17, 22, 45, 55
  top-down process 6, 17, 22, 45, 49, 55, 135
contrast 35–52, 95, 110, 126–7, 131–2, 134–5, 138–42, 144, 146, 148, 151–2, 154–5

Daniel, Frank 30, 35, 61, 72, 80, 157
deus ex machina 148–9, 153
dialogue
  conflict 101–3
  hook 67, 133, 139
  indirection 106, 110, 143, 146
  ironic 106–8, 110
  on the nose 105, 107–8
  subtext in 105–6
Double Indemnity (1944) 20, 25, 28, 49–50, 70, 101–3, 106

Empire (1964) 87
exposition 53–64, 87, 138
  information dump 53–4, 59, 63, 131, 133
  title crawl 54, 56–64, 132

Fellowship of the Ring, The (2001) 15, 36
Field, Syd 29, 93, 121, 136, 140
fixations 39, 51
Flash Gordon (1936) 54
Freytag, Gustav 35, 65, 93

Goldfinger (1964) 28
Gravity (2013) 150

Hangover, The (2009) 89
hero 19, 23, 28–9, 93, 121–3, 126–7, 136
hook questions 27, 33, 76
Howard, David 19, 53, 60, 72, 93–4

Still Alice (2014) 114
imagination 107, 111–19
  creativity 112–14
  left brain 112
  right brain 112
  stages 115–20
irony 106–9, 111

language comprehension 69
Lars and the Real Girl (2007) 25, 28
Lawrence of Arabia (1962) 37, 41–2, 72, 85–6, 104, 117
Lubitsch, Ernst 56, 106
Lucas, George 3, 35, 131, 149, 150

McKee, Robert 19, 23, 29–30, 55, 60, 93, 105–6, 114
memory 88
momentary relevance 43
Monty Python and the Holy Grail (1975) 128

neuronal fatigue 40–1
Ninotchka (1939) 56–60
nonvolitional processes 56
North By Northwest (1959) 47–9

object recognition 8, 17
One Flew Over the Cuckoo's Nest (1975) 20, 25, 28, 30, 103

Panksepp, Jaak 26, 71
perceptual salience 43
Phantom Menace, The (1999) 150
preparation (priming) 152–3
  by contrast 43
  part of creative process 114–15, 118
protagonist 19, 27–9, 33–4, 94, 109, 128, 134, 136
Psycho (1960) 34, 128, 137

rods 80

saccades 40, 51, 81, 115
Safety Last (1923) 21, 33
schemas (schematas) 8–9, 17, 22, 55, 59, 61–3, 127–8, 132, 136, 150
  frame 11, 17

scene 9, 17
script 11, 17
  violations of 9, 17
seeking 26–7, 33, 139
Seinfeld (1989–98) 90
sequences 94–5, 133, 137–9, 142, 151, 153
shared emotions 82, 90
Shop Around the Corner, The (1940) 65, 67–8, 73
short films, challenges of 89–90
Silver Linings Playbook (2012) 25, 28, 30, 59–60, 66, 72, 74, 94–5, 103
size constancy 77
Snyder, Blake 19, 23, 25, 30, 53–4, 93, 105, 122–3, 125–7, 136
Social Network, The (2010) 20, 42–3, 66–7, 70–2, 83, 86, 108
Some Like It Hot (1959) 13
Stalag 17 (1954) 73
Star Wars (1977) 3, 35–6, 46, 54, 61–2, 91, 125, 131–56
Strangers on a Train (1950) 81
Sundberg, Ingrid (diagram) 124

tension 11, 17, 36, 42, 45, 51, 94, 100, 125–7, 133–5, 137, 140, 143–4, 146, 151–2, 155–6
thalamus 69, 76
theme 30–1, 134
Thief of Baghdad, The (1922) 84
Toy Story (1995) 11, 30, 41, 73, 95, 107–8
tragic flaw (hamartia) 29
Trouble in Paradise (1932) 106–7

valences 45–9, 51, 135
virtual reality, challenges of 90–1
Vogler, Christopher (Writer's Journey structure) 28, 121–3, 126–7

working narrative 74